CONVERSATIONS
ON *Leadership*

Integrated Management
Resources Inc.

Compliments of
Greg Maciolek
Integrated Management Resources, Inc.
Phone: 865-675-5901 / Fax : 865-675-5907
Greg.Maciolek@imrtn.com
www.imrtn.com

Insight Publishing Company
Sevierville, Tennessee

Published by Insight Publishing Company
P.O. Box 4189
Sevierville, Tennessee 37864

10 9 8 7 6 5 4 3 2

Printed in the United States of America

ISBN: 1-885640-41-2

Table Of Contents

A Message From The Publisher

The mere fact that you are holding this book and reading this page says something about you. You must be a leader, aspire to become a leader or, at the very least, are curious about what makes a leader tick. You are, in fact, a rarity in this world, because real, honest-to-goodness leaders are not found on every street corner or behind every desk.

Real leaders are unique. They think differently. They see their world and their role in it differently. Most people see a problem and form an opinion. A leader sees a problem and begins formulating a plan. Most people wonder what their purpose is in life. A leader already knows.

I'm not saying that leadership is easy. In fact, it is not only difficult, it is often lonely and frustrating. Leaders are not perfect. Their flaws gnaw at them and at times bring them to ruin. But leaders never quit leading, and they should never quit learning about themselves and about leadership in an ever-changing world.

Conversations on Leadership is a collection of conversations from some of America's most dynamic leaders. Their insights, perspectives, and strategies are having a dramatic impact on people, organizations, and even countries, across America and around the world. You will learn from these leaders and find encouragement and inspiration to continue your own leadership journey. It is a journey well worth taking.

Interviews conducted by:

David E. Wright
President, International Speakers Network

Chapter 1

STEVE GILLILAND

THE INTERVIEW

David E. Wright (Wright)

Today we are speaking to Steve Gilliland. President and CEO of Performance Plus Professional Development, Inc.; a company dedicated to training, developing and improving people worldwide. His background includes major league baseball, broadcasting, and 11 years of corporate management. Steve's clients are a who's who list in American business and not-for-profit organizations. He is a member of the American Society for Training and Development, a professional member of the National Speakers Association, and is represented by the prestigious Washington Speakers Bureau. Steve Gilliland, welcome to *Conversations on Leadership*.

Steve Gilliland (Gilliland)

Hi, David. It's nice to be back on your program.

Wright

Steve, you've worked with some of the finest companies in America. As you've met with successful leaders in these companies, have you found any traits that they seem to have in common?

Gilliland

David, the two most common traits I have found in all great leaders are character and commitment. Character determines who you are while commitment shows people you have conviction. Some leaders have been blessed with talents, but character is a choice. It is more than talk. I have always defined character by your actions matching your beliefs. In addition, I believe that leaders cannot rise above the limitations of their character. If a leader's actions and intentions are continually working against each other, then I look at their character to find out why. Leaders with commitment stand out. They set goals, commit to them, and pay the price to reach them. Commitment opens the door to achievement and sometimes is the only thing that carries you forward when you face obstacles and adversity.

Wright

Many people have said that the difference between great managers and great leaders is vision. Have you found that to be true?

Gilliland

I have always operated from the premise that you must focus on the big picture and let others worry about the details. Another way of saying it is, "Leaders focus on the forest while managers focus on the trees." As a leader you have to cut through all the fog and smoke and identify what the key issues are. When you do this your subordinates (followers) feel encouraged that they are making progress. Priorities can be set and directives given because the leader sees the big picture.

Wright

So, being a great role model would be high on your list.

Gilliland

Most definitely! All great leaders must possess two things: values and vision. What I stand for, care about, and knowing where I am heading guides me and motivates other people.

Wright

Speaking of getting people to follow you, true leaders seem to be great communicators. What, in your opinion, is the most powerful communication tool a leader can use?

Gilliland

I would have to say telling an employee the truth with compassion. What I mean is, it's talking to people rather than about them and doing it in a respectful and caring way rather than a disdainful and condescending way. I find sometimes that people just enjoy being the boss too much. They kind of forget where they've come from. When I've spoken to educational groups, I've asked the question "Why is it that principals forget when they were a teacher and teachers forget when they were students?" We sometimes forget that our job is to coach, mentor, and grow people to reach their potential, not supervise them to see how many mistakes they make.

Wright

I've heard you speak to groups of professional people about enjoying their life both professionally as well as personally. What can leaders do to create an environment that allows talent and potential to develop, excitement about their jobs to occur, successful teams to develop and personal growth to happen?

Gilliland

Build trust, accentuate the positive, and redirect people when they make mistakes. The best way to create a great work environment is to build trust. The best way to build trust is to help people win and succeed at what they do. In addition, the best way to help people succeed at what they do is to not place too much energy and emphasis on their shortcomings. Withholding information without clear expectations, and treating everyone the same doesn't create the right environment. Trust is built when they know you care about them and they sense your eagerness to help them succeed. To accentuate the positive we need to focus more on praising progress and not achievement. And when mistakes occur we need to immediately redirect people in the right direction and stop dwelling on what they did wrong. The bottom line will always increase when you create the right work environment. Profit is the applause you receive from taking care of people.

Wright

Some employees have, and I've heard you talk about some of these people who have been through down times and they've had to struggle with the consequences of past mistakes and bad decisions in their life. Great leaders seem to get the best out of these people and motivate them to be better than they ever were. What do you think it takes to get the best out of people who have had these kinds of challenges?

Gilliland

Help them learn from adversity and teach them to find the opportunity in problems. As long as we maintain the right attitude and a certain amount of flexibility, we will be able to persist through the ups and downs we face in our day-to-day lives. The first step is to accept responsibility for your actions. You can't blame your failures on other people, nor can you blame it on fate. Next, you need to be willing to let go of your past and latch on to a new opportunity. Finally, our role as leaders is to help them envision something better. If they can see it, they will move towards it. I have always believed that problems will accelerate your growth as long as you see your problems as stepping stones to something better. If we can realize their purpose, our dependence, and be vulnerable, then we can take our past challenges and use them for our future successes.

Wright

That's great advice. In all the many books that you've read about leadership, who do you consider to be the greatest leaders in our history?

Gilliland

Without question, Abraham Lincoln and Martin Luther King, Jr. When we think we have it rough we need to remember that Abraham Lincoln, in only ten days before he took the oath of office in 1861, the Confederate States of America seceded from the union taking all Federal agencies, forts, and arsenals within their territory. To make matters worse, Lincoln, who was elected by a minority of the popular vote, was viewed by his own advisors as nothing more than a gawky, second-rate country lawyer with no leadership experience. The tumultuous times that he faced revealed his diverse leadership abilities. If you study Lincoln's leadership style it will help you lead in today's complex world. Then you look at the principles of Martin Luther King, Jr. and you sit in awe of someone who had the ability to speak the listener's language. He always gave credit where credit was due and when there were agonizing setbacks he was tolerant of mistakes. He gave us new thinking for a new era and made us all realize that creative new endeavors bring people together, unify them, and keep them focused. No two people in our history exemplified true leadership more than Abraham Lincoln and Martin Luther King Jr. When faced with extreme situations they used extreme remedies. They had the courage to stand alone and as they say...the rest is history.

Wright

If you were giving one piece of advice to someone who was just starting their leadership career, what would that single nugget be?

Gilliland

Become self-improving. The number one failure of many new leaders is that they are not teachable. Pride is a serious enemy of self-improvement. They need to put themselves in learning roles whenever possible. Instead of talking in meetings when people ask for advice, listen, and always ask questions anytime you don't understand something. If they can adopt an attitude of a learner and not an expert, they have a better chance. Also, they should plan their progress. If they are willing to identify their weak areas and then plan to improve they will. Too many times we take the "stick your head in sand" approach and are either blinded by our shortcomings or we make comparisons that falsely raise our worth. Finally, right from the "horses' mouth," value self-improvement over self promotion. Make your next career move based on how it will improve you personally rather than how it will enhance you financially.

Wright

Steve, you've written several development guidebooks and one of you're best sellers is on interviewing entitled, *Creaming the Crop*. What do you consider the key to hiring the best people?

Gilliland

Don't put too much stock in a person's resume. If you can, get someone else to screen it so you don't even see it. I think there are too many cracks in the resume that distort and bias your view of a person. I've always said it this way: The most important thing you should know about resumes is they are like mirrors in a fun house. They offer a distorted image of reality whose main function is to deceive the eye. I recently asked a group of head bank tellers, who were getting ready to hire some other tellers, this question, "What characteristics are you looking for in a teller?" They responded by saying,

"Friendly, personable, outgoing, good attitude... ." David, they named about six or seven things and what I found most interesting was this: Nothing they wanted in a teller could be found by looking at a resume. We spend too much energy and time in hiring people for what they know and eventually firing them for who they are. The key is simply to hire people for who they are. The interview process should be a thorough examination of a person's character and commitment.

Wright

What would you consider to be one of the most overlooked areas of leadership development today?

Gilliland

We don't train our leaders on how to coach, counsel, and mentor the various generations that now work within our organizations. There has always been the problem of communication, but now the bar has been raised with the influx of generation "x" and "y." Traditionalists and Baby Boomers are realizing that what worked in the 90's may not work in the new millennium. Leaders drive their people crazy and even worse, don't know why. You show me a leader who is flexible, develops their people, involves them, walks the talk, and remembers that leadership is not brain surgery, and I will show you someone who is a strong communicator to all generations in the workplace.

Wright

What, in your opinion, is the difference between management and leadership?

Gilliland

A manager administers; the leader innovates. A manager is a copy; the leader is original. A manager maintains; the leader develops. A manager asks how and when; the leader asks what and why. A manager accepts status quo; the leader challenges status quo. A manager has their eye on the bottom line; the leader has their eye on the horizon. A manager focuses on structure; the leader focuses on people. A manager relies on control; the leader inspires trust. A manager has a short-range view; the leader has a long range perspective. A manager does things right; the leader does the right thing. Leaders always touch a persons heart before they ask for their hand. They always love their people more than their position. Most of all a leader develops themselves to become the person others will follow.

Wright

So, you think they've got to do both to be successful?

Gilliland

I think it always depends on the circumstances. The real key is to chart the course and then let them steer the ship.

Wright

What would you consider to be the greatest book that you've ever read on the subject of leadership?

Gilliland

I would have to say one that stands out is Steven Covey's, *Principle Centered Leadership*. He's also the author of, *The 7 Habits of Highly Effective People*. His philosophy for creating more meaningful relationships and successes in the workplace is a strategy that we should be striving to implement throughout business and industry, organizations, our homes and everywhere. I think there are people like Sam Walton, the chairman of Wal-Mart Stores, and a lot of other people that have based their businesses and the direction of their business on this principle centered leadership. I believe Steven Covey is the one that said, "Give a man a fish and you can feed him for a day. Teach him how to fish and you can feed him for a lifetime." Covey's principles are timeless and if followed can lead to a very rewarding life, both personally and professionally.

Wright

You know, to digress a second, when I see leaders on television, whether they're in interviews or even on these programs where these lawyers work day and night, you're always seeing them back in their offices at one or two o'clock in the morning still working. You read their resume of all the Men of the Year type things they've won or the Woman of the Year, and it seems like the list of things they're involved in are just endless. I often wonder when do they take time to rest and relax, to be with their families and that sort of thing? I heard you talking about enjoying the ride at a conference and I said, "can you really be a great leader and really sustain without enjoying the things that perhaps God intended you to enjoy?"

Gilliland

Well, I believe it's like anything else in life, you have to strike a balance. Achieving balance in your personal and professional life is no easy task. When you do, it leads to richer relationships, longer life, happiness, enjoyment, and inner peace. I mention in my book, *Enjoy The Ride,* "Many people believe that once you arrive at wherever your "there" is, you will finally become happy, generous, loving, and content. What happens is that you constantly long for something else and never allow yourself the joy of the present." I believe that balance is accomplished when you are focused on what you have right now, the important things, while simultaneously holding the intention of your future goals. When you put the future ahead of the present you begin to lose your balance.

Wright

I've often wondered, people like you who do a tremendous amount of traveling in your schedules are always busy, you're flying from one place to the other, do you ever get to take any one or more of your family to these places you go.

Gilliland

I do. Ironically my oldest son, Stephen, who works in the business with us, just recently worked a trade show with me in Myrtle Beach. I also had him attend a conference in Las Vegas where I spoke to the National Association of Educational Buyers. My youngest son Josh doesn't like to fly, so sometimes Josh has accompanied me on trips that doesn't require a plane. I am very fortunate that my sons have not only accompanied me, but have also been part of what I do when they attend. My mother and stepfather have heard me speak several times. Of course, she is my biggest fan and would travel full time if she was able to. As a matter of fact, she is quite the speaker, so maybe I should incorporate her in some of my seminars. The morning I leave on any trip, my mother and I get together for coffee at her house (my stepfather grinds the beans fresh) and we discuss my trip, have a little prayer, and then I'm on my way. I am a firm believer that we need to take time to share a moment with our families, because it is the foundation for your memories.

Wright

So, as I read this conversation, you're actually implementing what you're talking about as a leader. You're trying to find a balance, you're trying to help other people; the things that you talked about in leadership, seems like to me, you're doing yourself.

Gilliland

I try. I was just recently interviewed and asked, "What's the biggest challenge in what you do as a professional speaker?" and I said, "Actually living the message that I speak and trying to make sure that it's something that I adhere to myself. I really believe that your audience can never become something you're not. I think that's the same with parenting and with leading people. I don't think people that work for you can become something you're not. I believe you have such an influence over them that they're going to watch what you're going to do a whole lot more than listen to what you say.

Wright

Well, it seems to be working. I have an office manager that when she talks to the staff, she says "As Steve Gilliland would say..." They say, "Oh not again!"

Gilliland

That's very flattering!

Wright

I think to myself, "Could you not quote me once in a while?" Who influenced your leadership career the most?

Gilliland

Without question my mother, my brother, and my former secretary. My mother is the epitome of the transparent leader. She is what she is and stands for what she believes. She never doubts her beliefs and isn't afraid to stand alone. She is also very compassionate towards people. My mother has taught me to be a giver and not a taker and is a real example of what servant leadership is all about. As for my brother Kim, he exemplifies the words character and integrity. He too stands up for what he believes, and is unwavering when it comes to doing what is right and always telling the truth. His love for his wife and children can't be measured. I firmly believe he is the model husband and father. And finally, my former secretary Margaret, who taught me so much about life and leadership, greatly influenced my leadership career. She taught me to love my people more than my position, and also made me realize the difference between leadership and management. I have been very blessed to have a mother, stepfather, brother, and secretary who have always stood beside me and have been great role models for me.

Wright

Well, what a great conversation! I've certainly learned a lot and I want you to know how much I appreciate you taking this much time to talk to me today.

Gilliland

David, I enjoyed our time together and look forward to the next time.

Wright

Today we have been talking to Steve Gilliland. He is the President and CEO of Performance Plus Professional Development, Inc., a company dedicated to training, developing and improving people worldwide. As we have found out this morning, he's pretty good at it. Thank you so much for being with us on *Conversations on Leadership*, Steve.

Gilliland

Thank you, so much, David. The pleasure was mine.

About The Author

Since the turn of the century, Steve Gilliland has become one of the most sought-after speakers in America. His background includes Major League Baseball, broadcasting, and eleven years of corporate management on three different levels. Steve has experienced what others merely talk about. He is the President and CEO of Performance Plus Professional Development, Inc., a Pittsburgh, Pennsylvania-based company recognized by the Pittsburgh Business Times as one of the top training companies in Western Pennsylvania. Whether he is kicking off an event, training all day, or closing a convention, Steve Gilliland is not only a speaker who challenges people to change, he motivates them to do so. His audiences and clients are a who's who list in American business and not-for-profit organizations.

Steve Gilliland

Performance Plus

PO Box 4182

Pittsburgh, Pennsylvania 15202

Phone: 877.499.8901

Fax: 412.766.8998

Email: steveg@performanceplus1.com

www. stevegilliland.com

Chapter 2

DR. WARREN BENNIS

THE INTERVIEW

David E. Wright (Wright)

Today we are talking with Dr. Warren Bennis. He is a university professor and a distinguished professor of business at the University of Southern California and chairman of USC's leadership institute. He has written 18 books, including *On Becoming A Leader, Why Leaders Can't Lead,* and *The Unreality Industry,* co-authored with Ivan Mentoff. Dr. Bennis was successor to Douglas McGregor as chairman of the organizational studies department at MIT. He also taught at Harvard and Boston Universities. Later he was provost and executive vice president of the State University of NY—Buffalo and president of the University of Cincinnati. He published over 900 articles and two of his books have earned the coveted McKenzie Award for the "Best Book on Management." He has served in an advisory capacity for the past four U.S. presidents, and consultant to many corporations and agencies and to the United Nations. Awarded 11 honorary degrees, Dr. Bennis has also received numerous awards including the distinguished service award of the American Board of Professional Psychologists and the Perry L. Ruther practice award of the American Psychological Association. Dr. Bennis, welcome to *Conversations on Leadership.*

Dr. Warren Bennis (Bennis)

I'm glad to be here again with you, David.

Wright

In a conversation with *Behavior Online*, you stated that most organizations devaluate potential or emerging leaders by seven criteria: business literacy, people skills, conceptual abilities, track record, taste, judgment, and character. Because these terms were somewhat vague, you left them to be defined by the reader. Can we give our readers an unadorned definition of these criteria, as you define them?

Bennis

There's no precise dictionary definition that would satisfy me or maybe anyone. I'll just review them very quickly because there's a lot more we want to discuss. Business literacy really means: do you know the territory, do you know the ecology of the business, do you know how it works, do you know where the plugs are, do you know who the main stakeholders are, and are you familiar with a thing called business culture. People skills: This is your capacity to connect and engage, because business leadership is about establishing, managing, creating and engaging in relationships. Conceptual abilities is more important these days because it has to do with the paradoxes and complexities; the cartography of stakeholders that make life at the top (more than ever) interesting and difficult, which is why we've had such a turnover in CEOs and leaders over the last few years. Track record: Now, if I want to know about a person, if I were a therapist, one of the first questions I would ask is, "Tell me about your job history." That tells me a lot. On the whole, as my dad used to say, "People who get A's are smart." People who have a successful track record tend to be effective. We don't always go on that, because sometimes these people don't grow. But, if I had only one measuring stick, it would be that one: Tell me your job history. Let's talk about whether it looks successful or whether the person views it as successful or not. It's hard to define, but it's about whether or not you have the capacity a good curator has, a good selector has, to know people. It's always a tough one, God knows we all make mistakes. Your taste means your capacity to judge other people in relation to the other six characteristics. I think, taste and judgment are combined. I dealt with them separately because I thought taste was specifically the selection of people in an intuitive and objective way, but also in a subjective way. It has to do with the range of such things as being bold vs. being reckless. It has to do with the strategic implications and consequences of any decision and what you take into account in making any decision, especially the tough ones. The easy ones are different; everyone looks good in a bull market. It's when things get tough, vulnerable, difficult and in a crisis mode that judgment really counts the most. Taste and judgment are the hardest things to learn, let alone teach. Character: Here I have in mind a variety of things such as size of ego, the capacity to listen, emotional intelligence, integrity and authenticity. Basically, is this a person I can trust? That's what character is all about.

Wright

You said that businesses get rid of their top leaders because of lapses in judgment, lapses in character, not because of business literacy or conceptual skills. Why do you think this is true?

Bennis

It's true simply because it's true. Look at the record. I wasn't just stating a hypothesis there that looks to be proved. I was stating experiences with leaders, and I'll give you three quick examples. Let's look at a recent one. Howell Raines—the top job in journalism in the world—had great ideas, great business literacy, all the things in the top five. He did not have taste, judgment, or character. This is a guy who had an ego the size of Texas. He played favorites, had the best ideas, was a terrific newspaper man and no one would argue with that. But, his way of treating people, of not harnessing the human harvest that was there, and being bullying and brutalizing and arrogant and unable to listen; that's what I mean by character. Eckhart Pfeiffer was fired after seven or eight very good years at Compaq—he had terrific ideas, but he did not listen to the people. He was only listening to his "A" list, who were saying, "Aye, aye, Sir." His "B" list was saying, "You better look at what Gateway and Dell are doing; they're eating our lunch on our best china." He didn't listen; he didn't want to listen. That's what I mean by character. Let me just stay with those two examples, I don't think it's ever about conceptual abilities, ever. There may be some examples I don't know about. But, with over fifty years of leadership research, I don't know of any leader who has lost his job or has been ousted because of a lack of brain power.

Wright

You said that teaching leadership is impossible, but you also said leadership can be learned. How can that be?

Bennis

Let me qualify that. I teach the stuff, so no, it isn't impossible to teach you. As is the case with everything, teaching and learning are two different things. One has to do with input into people; the other has to do with whether or not they get it. You know very well, and your listeners and readers know very well, that there's a difference between listening to a lecture and it having any influence on you. You can listen to a brilliant lecture and nothing may happen. So, there's a disconnect to teaching and learning. Actually, how people learn about leadership varies a lot. Most people don't learn about leadership by a Ph.D., or by reading a book, or by listening to this tape, although that may be helpful; they learn it through work and experience. You can be helped by terrific teaching, like a recording, like a tape, like a book, like a weekend retreat. Basically, the way people learn about leadership is by keeping their eyes open, being a first class observer, having good role models and being able to see how they deal with life's adversities. You don't learn leadership by reading books; they are helpful, don't get me wrong. I write books; I want them to be read. The message you are trying to get out to your people, to listen to and to read is also important. I think it's terrific. That's my life's work. That's what I do for a living, and I love it. I'll tell you, it has to be augmented by the experiences you face in work and in life.

Wright

Trust me, I have learned after reading many of your books that they are teaching materials.

Bennis

Thank-you. I hope you also learn from them, David.

Wright

As I was reading those books, I wondered why I did the things you said to do, and they worked when I did it. It's simply because I learned by doing.

Bennis

Thank-you. I'm really glad to hear that.

Wright

Since leadership is where the big money, prestige and power is, why would seasoned business executives, who are monitored more closely than the average employee, let character issues bring them down? One would think it would be like a person who constantly uses profanity, just deciding not to curse in church.

Bennis

I wish it were that easy. It's a really good question. I wish I knew the answer, but I don't. I will give you a real quick example. Howell Raines, as I said before, executive editor of the New York Times—people would die to get that position—was an experienced newspaper man, and there was a 17,000 word article about him in New Yorker, June 6, 2002 (he had been on the job since Sept. 2001, so it was written not a year later). The article exposed him; it was a very frank and interesting article. It called him arrogant, a bully, playing favorites, all the things I said earlier, and also called him a hell of a good man and a terrific editor. He'd been around the track; he had business literacy up the wah-zoo. He was as good as they get. He read that article and everybody at the New York Times read it. Do you think it might have made him want to change a little bit? Did Julius Caesar not hear the warnings, "Beware the Ides of March?" Did he not hear, "Don't go to the forum?" There were so many signals and he wasn't listening. Why wasn't he listening? Didn't he go down to the newsroom and talk to those people? No. The most common and fatal error, is that because of arrogance; they stopped listening. It could happen internally, as in the case of Howell Raines, or like Eckhart Pfeiffer, who wasn't listening to his "D" list tell him about Gateway and Dell. I don't have the answer to your question, but I will tell you, someone ought to be around to remind these people of the voices, stakeholders and audiences that they aren't listening to. That's a way of dealing with it; making sure you have a trusted staff that isn't just giving you the good news.

Wright

I've often heard that if I had been Nixon, I would have burned the tapes, apologized, and moved on.

Bennis

Absolutely.

Wright

I think it's the arrogance factor; you really hit the nail on the head when you said that, to put it in my simple terms. How does one experience leadership when they haven't yet become a leader?

Bennis

How do you become a parent for the first time? There's no book that you are going to read on becoming a parent any more than there is a book you are going to read on becoming a leader that will prepare you for that experience. You're going to fall on your face, get up, dust yourself off, and go on. The only thing you're going to learn from is your experiences and having someone around you that you can depend on for straight, reflective back talk. A lot of it is breaks, it is chance. Some of it isn't that, but if there's one thing I want to underscore, nobody is prepared the first time they are going to be in the leadership position. You're going to fall on your face, you're going to learn from it, and you're going to continue that for the rest of your life.

Wright

At one time, I had a company with about 175 people working for me; we had business in the millions. I just kept making so many mistakes that afterward, I did wish that I had read some of the things you had written about before I made those mistakes. It sure would have been helpful. In your studies, you found that failure, not success, had a greater impact on future leaders, that leaders learn the most by facing adversity. Do you think this is made clear by teachers at the college level?

Bennis

I can't speak for all teachers at the college level. Do you mean people teaching leadership and business management at the college level?

Wright

Yes.

Bennis

I don't know if they do. But, I would imagine things are much more difficult and complicated today because of the kinds of things that business leaders are facing such as: globalization, fierce Darwinian competitiveness, the complexity of the problems, the regulatory pressures, the changes in demography, the difficulty of retaining your best talent, the price of terrific human capital and then keeping them, the ability to help create a climate that encourages collaboration, and then there's the world danger since 9/11.

Wright

In my case, I just remember the equations and things in the courses I took, like controlling and directing and those kinds of things, and I don't remember anybody ever telling me about exit strategies or what's going to happen if my secretary gets pregnant and my greatest salesperson is the one responsible for it. Who do I fire? As the owner of a small company that's growing at a rapid pace, what can I do to facilitate the competencies of the people I have chosen to lead this into the future?

Bennis

Your company is how big, again?

Wright

I was talking before about a real estate conglomerate. Presently I have a speakers bureau/servicing agency and publishing business, and employ about 25 people, and we also use about 50 vendors, which I look at as employees.

Bennis

Yes, they are, aren't they? That's a good way of thinking about it. There are several things you can do in any size company, but with a small company, you can get your arms around it, conceptually, anyway. The leader/owner has to model the very behaviors that he wants others to model; if you are espousing something that is antithetical to your behavior, then that's going to be a double bind. That's number one. The second thing is to make leadership development an organic part of the activities at the firm. In addition to encouraging people to read, bringing in people to talk to them and having retreats, every once in a while, look at leadership competencies and what people can do to sharpen and enhance into those capacities that are needed to create a culture where people can openly talk about these issues. All of those things can be used to create a climate where leadership development is a part of the everyday dialogue.

Wright

If you were helping me choose people to assume leadership roles as my company grows, what characteristics would you suggest I look for?

Bennis

I've implied some of them early on, as we discussed those seven characteristics. I've become a little leery of the whole selection process; there is some evidence that even interviews don't give you really valid insight. I think what I would tend to do is look at the track record. Talk about that with the person, where they think they have failed, where they think they have succeeded. Try to get a sense of their capacity to reflect on issues and see to what extent they have been able to learn from their previous experiences. See what you can make of how realistically they assess a situation. Most people rarely attribute any blame to themselves; they always think, "the dog ate my homework." It's always some other agent outside of themselves who is to blame. Those are the things that I think are going to be characteristics of emerging leaders among men and women. That's what I would look for, the capacity to reflect and learn.

Wright

When you made that comment about interviews, I don't feel as inept as I did before this conversation. I'm 64 years old and the longer I live, I just feel that when people come in and interview, I want to give them an Academy Award as they walk out. People can say almost anything convincingly in this culture. It's very, very difficult for me to get through, so that's one thing I really had not thought of. It seems so simple; just follow the track record.

Bennis

I have had the same experience as you. When I was president of the university and making lots of choices all the time, my best was hitting 700, which means I was off three out of ten times. I think my average here was 60/40; it's rough. It's even harder these days because of legal restrictions, how much you can say about their references, how much they can reveal. We have to pay attention to selection level, no kidding. We can overcome mistakes in the selection level by the culture and how it will screen out behaviors that are not acceptable. That's our best default; the culture itself will so educate people that even mistakes we make will be resurrected by the culture being our best friend and ally.

Wright

As a leader, generating trust is essential. You have written extensively on this subject. Can you give our readers some factors that tend to generate trust?

Bennis

People want a leader that exudes that they know what he/she is doing. They want a doctor who is competent; they want a boss who really knows their way around. Secondly, you want someone who is really on your side; a caring leader. Thirdly, you want a leader who has directness, integrity, congruity, they return calls and are trustworthy. They will be there when needed and they do care about you and they do care about your growth. Those are the main things. It's not just individuals involved. A boss must create a climate within the group that provides psychological safety, a holding pattern where people feel comfortable in speaking openly. I think that's another key factor in generating and establishing trust.

Wright

It is said that young people these days have less hope than their parents. What can leaders do to instill hope in their employees?

Bennis

All, and you can underline all, the leaders I have known have a high degree of optimism and a low degree of pessimism. They are, as Confucius said, purveyors of hope. Look at Reagan, in a way look at Clinton or Martin Luther King Jr.; these are people who have held out an idea of what we could become and made us proud of ourselves, created noble aspirations, sometimes audacious, but noble. Leaders have to express in an authentic way that there is a future for our nation and that you have a part in developing that future with me.

Wright

Dr. Bennis, thank you for being with us today, and for taking so much time to answer these questions.

Bennis

Thank-you for having me.

About The Author

Warren Bennis has written or edited twenty-seven books, including the best-selling *Leaders* and *On Becoming A Leader*, both of which have been translated into twenty-one languages. He has served on four U.S. presidential advisory boards and has consulted for many Fortune 500 companies, including General Electric, Ford and Starbucks. *The Wall Street Journal* named him one of the top ten speakers on management in 1993 and 1996, and *Forbes* magazine referred to him as "the dean of leadership gurus."

Warren Bennis
m.christian@marshall.usc.edu

Chapter 3

MIKE FOTI

THE INTERVIEW

David E. Wright (Wright)

Today we are talking with Mike Foti who is the Chief Executive Officer of Cleveland Glass Block, Inc., as well as a leader and owner in seven additional partnerships and corporations. Mike is a successful entrepreneur with construction and real estate businesses with located from the East Coast to the Rockies where sales have grown over 330% over the past 10 years. One of Mike's companies, Cleveland Glass Block, was awarded the North Coast 99 Award as a best employer in Northeast Ohio and the Community Pillar Award for service. Mike began his career with Cleveland Twist Drill and progressed to be the youngest Product Manager at the age of 24. He purchased his first corporation, Cleveland Glass Block, when he was 25 years old. He has an MBA from Case Western Reserve University (ranked as a top ten school in the world for entrepreneurship) and a B.S. in Business Administration from Carnegie-Mellon University. Mike is active on non-profit and for profit boards in the areas of regional development, education, and construction. These organizations include the Institute for Educational Renewal, Graduates Council, Council of Smaller Enterprises, Ohio Business Week Foundation, Cuyahoga County Reemployment Service Center, and Nelson Homes.

Mike is also a previous board member and leader of the membership and operations functions of the National Speakers Association of Ohio. Mr. Foti, welcome to *Conversations on Leadership.*

Mike Foti (Foti)
Thank you.

Wright
Mike, you talk in your speaking programs about the need to *"evolve"* as a leader. What do you mean by this and how would someone go about this process?

Foti
To *evolve* you must <u>stop</u>. Hard to believe, but to move forward you first must freeze dead in your tracks, then ask yourself three simple, yet critical questions. First, "What do you <u>love to do</u>?" Second, "What are you <u>good at</u>?" Where are your competencies and skills, and where can you make the most powerful contribution? Third, "Where is there a <u>need</u>—in the market, the community and the world for what you have to offer?" While you may love to do something and may be good at it, if there is no need, the first two questions are irrelevant! Great leaders look for and reflect on "the intersection" of these 3 questions. Then they dig in and courageously take action!

The problem, as I see it, is that we are sometimes blinded to our own strengths. What you may perceive as "easy" may actually be your best area to focus on—what you are "good at." Your best area of *evolution* may be where people are asking for your help—wanting to draw upon your expertise. I recommend people look for times where their excitement in a project makes it seem like time is flying. This would be an indication of what they "love to do."

I believe all people are in one of 3 "states"—*evolving, revolving, or dissolving.* The smallest, select group consists of people evolving. It takes a conscious effort, risk, a sense of focus and purpose to evolve. It is a challenging journey, not a final destination! *"Revolving"* is what's natural and predominant for most. We are habitual. We tend to get coffee at the same place every day, keep the same routine. We revolve and create a pattern in our lives. The last group of people is *"dissolving."* They may be in a tough place in life, feel like a victim of circumstances, and may not be see themselves as responsible for their own situation. Often, life just seems to get worse for people who are "dissolving."

Wright

Mike, with your experience how do you inspire and motivate those people you lead that are *"revolving"* (stuck in their habits) to improve both individual and team results?

Foti

I have found successful leaders improve individual results by **not focusing on retention!** Yes, I know Human Resource professional's eyes are probably bulging out right now! The general business buzz says, we need to "retain" our people, but I have found the **important focus is to inspire**, not retain. Inspiration is what catapults the results of those who are revolving. It is about moving people to a higher level in their development and improving results. To do this, you need to coach, help them *where they are at this moment*, and not necessarily where we wish they should be. Increase the focus on individual "responsibilities" and de-emphasize "rights" of the position.

In my consulting and in my businesses, I challenge people to stop "revolving" by asking, "What are you doing *exceptionally* right now? What's something *exceptional* you can do today? What is something *exceptional* you are planning next week?" Most people who revolve are "busy" in their work, but rarely ask what they can do differently, or better, to provide a higher quality outcome. This is a practical and explosive way to create leadership growth.

Although individual results are important, great things happen through teams. I have found exceptional people have two seemingly paradoxical qualities. First, they are *unique*. They develop a "personal brand" and are not afraid to express their individuality through work. Paradoxically they are also able to *integrate* their uniqueness within the team's goals. So, when I'm working with someone who is revolving, I'll ask them to identify their uniqueness and how they can mesh their special skills into the goals of their work team.

Wright

What do you do about those who are *"dissolving?"*

Foti

The key question to ask is: Do they take responsibility for where they are, and are they willing to get off ground zero and move in a new direction? It took me 37 years to stop investing my time in people who had "potential," but would neither take responsibility nor the initiative to change. If responsibility and initiative are not present, I would move these people out of the organization ASAP!

Wright

That's a lesson most leaders learn reluctantly. I came from a strong Christian background and remember a fellow in Texas told me, "David you cannot reach down into the muck of life and pull up people who do not want to come."

Foti

You're right about that.

Wright

I argued mentally with that for 20 years, but finally figured out he was right. Baseball coaches, football coaches, they work to make people better and will give very little time to people who aren't trying. Mike, you've been quoted as saying "leadership evolution" requires *much more* than pure knowledge alone. It requires wisdom that can be applied to generate results. Given that we are progressively a knowledge-based economy, why do you make this comment?

Foti

If you look at our world right now, we have an explosion of knowledge. Information is doubling every 18 months, and is globally available through the Internet. A leaders' goal *is not* to get the most information! Those with the most facts don't necessarily win. The key to move from knowledge to results-generating wisdom first begins when you focus on where your leadership can have impact. Second, ask how you can "go deep" in your learning and use this knowledge to create tangible results. Finally, how can you coach others in your organization to replicate this wisdom?

A common saying is, "it's not what you know, it's who you know." I think this statement is garbage! *It is what we know.* If you look at somebody you respect, is it solely because they know so many influential people? Probably not. The real reason you hold them in high esteem is likely because they influenced your thinking with their knowledge, insights, wisdom, and results. I think most of us want to be respected in this way. To become this type of person we need to go deeper in our learning. Ask, "What new niche or slice of expertise can differentiate me?" Challenging yourself to simultaneously go deep in this niche <u>and</u> broaden your perspective—go deeper with content, and broader with context.

Why do we need to broaden our perspective? Because we're all 100% correct......from our point of view. Unfortunately, we don't always see the big picture. This can cause us to have what I call leadership "blind spots." Winning leaders open their minds. They start by *reflecting* on daily wins and losses, maximizing their learning and imparting this knowledge in others to create a ripple effect. They are willing to *experiment*, and ask, "What can I do to stretch my skills, and perform 'on the edge' of my comfort zone?"

I challenge leaders to stop focusing on "getting an education" and start "taking an education!" Don't see education as getting a degree from a university or attending training classes. To thrive today, it's wise to develop a personal learning plan and focus on how to *differentiate and integrate* your skills for results. As Warren Bennis would say, learn to be "whole brained." Create a plan to improve your critical thinking with "left brain" development. Also educate your "right brain" about communication, empathy, and creativity. Successful leadership evolution is about expanding the capacity of the entire brain and creating a personalized leadership development plan.

Wright

You're right about the comment—"it's not what you know, it's who you know." I've always thought that was an excuse for people who won't take the time to learn their craft. In my life, it's been "who knows you because of what you know."

Foti

Exactly! If you take time to "go deep" in your knowledge base <u>and</u> you get results, people will *seek you out*! It's not just knowledge for knowledge's sake. There are plenty of "smart" people in the world. But, the truly "smart" leader knows how to apply that learning in the <u>*real world*</u> to create a <u>*real result*</u>. It doesn't matter whether that's in an organization, a civic or social sector group, or your family—the technique is the same.

Wright

Mike, you believe the key to personal leadership success is to *"give help and get help."* First, how do you determine whom you give your time to?

Foti

First, I ask specifically where a person needs help to ensure I'm a good match. I'll ask, "What do you want to accomplish with our time together?" I'll ask them to send me a list of questions before we meet. This provides me with a context of where I might provide assistance, and helps me prepare so I am more useful than if I just tried to "wing it." I offer to make introductions to others who may be able to help as well. In this way, I'm a "conduit" for the goals and interests of others.

Wright

Where do you look for help? How do you make the most of the mentoring you receive?

Foti

I focus first on people who know what I need to know and who deliver their results with integrity. I look to make the most of my mentoring relationships by challenging myself to learn and grow beyond my current knowledge base and beyond the way I currently see the world. I love the quote from Satchel Paige (a pitcher for the Cleveland Indians in the 1940's) who said, "It's not what you know that will hurt you, it's what you know that just ain't so." The question is how can I stretch myself to be open to new viewpoints and listen to critical advice.

Wright

Mike, I know you believe one of the keys to effective leadership is being a "quiet leader." What is a "quiet leader" and why is this so important in today's results focused leadership environment? Can this type of leadership be developed?

Foti

When people think of leaders, the natural tendency is to gaze upward—to find a hero. People like Lee Iacocca and Donald Trump are charismatic, larger-than-life figures. Obviously, those leaders have many excellent qualities, but it has been researched (read article by Jim Collins titled, *Level 5 Leadership*) that consistently superior results are generated by leaders who combine two seemingly paradoxical qualities—*humility* and *delivery*. These are the top qualities of a "quiet leader."

A humble leader is someone who doesn't always absorb the spotlight (and take all the credit), but who reflects the spotlight (by recognizing and rewarding the contributions of the team). They understand their results are *interdependent* on others. When the spotlight clicks on, they reflect this attention to their team. The "quiet leader" also encourages honest feedback and asks, "What am I doing well? What am I not doing well? Where can I help you? Where can I remove obstacles to increase your personal success and your team's outcomes?"

The "quiet leader" lays a golden pathway for excellence. How? They help others develop two elements of their "personal gold." They are "gold plating" and "solid gold." Your "gold plating" is your image. It's how people initially judge you. Unfortunately, in our society your image ("gold plating") *does matter*. We need to know whether our image helps or hinders our ability to influence results. If it is a deterrent, the "evolving leader" will get advice from those "in the know," and make the needed changes to remove this obstacle.

A progressive leader also needs to work on their "solid gold"—their character. Excellent leaders should challenge themselves to become a "Mother Theresa in a UPS uniform." That's someone who demonstrates their leadership character through *service and delivery,* and ask the following questions: "How can I be of service? How can I make things easier for you? How can I create a result that won't simply benefit me, but will benefit my customer or the community?"

Obviously, a leader needs to <u>deliver</u>. They need to ask, "How can I deliver on my commitments? Are my words and actions integrated? Do I have a delivery system that gets consistent results? Does my team follow up and follow through?" The reality is, people hear what we say (if we're lucky), but they watch *intently* what we deliver. Rhetoric and inspirational messages only go so far. Ultimately, it boils down to results! A "quiet leader" creates an inspirational environment through their actions, service, delivery and "solid gold."

Wright

Mike, growing an organization requires *developing a vision*, a larger context and perspective for your leadership decisions. How do you accomplish this goal?

Foti

Visioning begins with simplification. Today, we're inundated with information and we're often overwhelmed with data, goals and objectives. Visioning can begin by creating a simple metaphor, a simple model, to guide our direction. In my Ohio-based glass block business we analyzed our current market position and determined we where a "big fish in a small pond" (i.e. #1 or #2 market share position with our niche product). The business was not growing fast enough to create the opportunities and returns we wanted. We looked at this situation and said, "That's where we are today, but what is our goal for tomorrow?" Our new vision is to go from being a "big fish in our small glass block pond" to become a "larger fish in the home services ocean that adds value to our customers and community." This vision provides a simplified picture of our future and also an aspirational context for how we plan to evolve.

A powerful vision should make sense to your team and should be based on the realities of the marketplace. We need to openly and honestly ask, "What are our trends, challenges and opportunities? How do we leverage our reality and help customers do something better?" How can we stand out and be "remarkable" to our customers? An active vision begins with focusing on the truth. Deception is the enemy of effective leadership. A leader plays a key role in defining reality and inspiring the team to catch the vision and run with it.

Wright

Mike, you define leadership as the ability to get results through others. In our fast-moving world, *creativity* and *innovation* will be key elements to create competitive advantage and get the high level of results for success. How do you grow these key skills in your business?

Foti

Creativity and innovation begin by **forgetting** the following line from the movie Apollo 13: "Failure *is not* an option!" Oh yes it is! In business, failure is not only an option; it's *critical* to success. We need to challenge ourselves to try creative new approaches. If your organization penalizes those who try and fail, odds are you can forget about employees risking their security to be innovative. To spur creativity, we need to create an environment where people know it's OK to fail (just not OK to fail repeatedly). It's OK to take a risk.

One approach I use to get the creative juices flowing is to share stories, but not the ones that make you look like a hero. Consider telling a personal story of a failure that hurt your bottom line. I have shared a story of a concrete paving stone installation business I owned with my brother. We lost a substantial sum of money. After telling the story I will say, "Now here's the tough lessons I learned from this business (1) give the business a certain amount of time to succeed (2) know how much cash you are willing to "invest" (this is the nice term for lose!), and (3) if you have a big, ugly brother named Frank—don't get into business with him! (a little humor to lighten things up). When our employees hear of my loss they probably think, "If Foti lost that much money it must be okay for me to try something new and take a risk as well!" Well, at least I _hope_ that's what they're thinking. Point is, use your "negative story" to open up risk taking.

Innovation also requires people who *"go to the fan"* (these are people who take initiative to run toward problems and not away from them). When big problems occur, most people don't go "to the fan," (toward the problem) they scurry away from it. They are either uncertain of their skills or feel they will be chastised if results don't match someone else's expectations. In our organization we try to celebrate people who take initiative. Creative problem solving presents a tremendous opportunity. Share "positive stories" of people who "go to the fan" in your organization. Make sure to celebrate, embrace and recognize the risk-takers in your organization!

Wright

Getting results through people would logically begin with having the right people in the first place. As a winner of the North Coast 99 Best Places to work, how does your organization make sure to get the right people in the right place? Also, how do you inspire a higher level of results?

Foti

Two ways. First, I'll go back to something we talked about previously. The leader's goal is not to achieve 100% retention; it's to strive for *100% inspiration.* Do we create an environment with 100% inspired people? No, that's not realistic. The challenge is to keep reaching for this goal. It starts with developing exciting work assignments where we match talent with work that needs done and inspire "evolving" people. Ask, "What do you love to do? What are you good at? Where is there a need?" I suggest you look at your current staff, ask those three questions, and match people to where they can have the biggest impact on both the business and their personal growth. Combine where you need help and where your employees want to grow.

Second, evaluate your *hiring process*. In recruiting, we look at two things. First: competency. We get very detailed with what specifically, practically and tangibly is expected from the position. We don't just look at the duties, but the expected results as well. Can this person deliver? Second (an often overlooked area) is hiring for values. It's hiring *for character*, not the first "characters" that walk through the door! We ask open-ended questions like, "What bugs you? What matters to you? Who has taught you the most?" We're trying to *understand the candidate* as a person. We realize that we want results from this new person, but we also want to know if their values can be integrated into our team. We want a unique person who will work *with us, not for us*. We don't work in silos. We recognize great things happen only through teams.

Wright

Results obviously don't happen by accident. As a Chief Executive Officer of five businesses in widely disbursed physical locations, what lessons have you learned from building these businesses: not only keeping it together, but thriving on a daily basis? What would you do differently if you could turn back the clock?

Foti

A key lesson I've learned in evaluating talent is that being nice is not necessarily correlated with being effective. No matter how "nice" a person may be, life isn't good if they don't get results! Determine whether the person is taking responsibility for what they need to accomplish and whether they are achieving results. Being a "nice" leader can also be problematic. Not directly addressing non-productive employees is extremely destructive to business results. Develop a specific plan for improvement, set up milestones to measure progress, and make changes if things don't improve.

I've also learned to have clear expectations and develop accountability. What specifically do we expect from someone and when do we expect results? Lets face it, in most organizations messages are muddy. Do we state clearly what we need? Do we ask the person how they feel about delivering these goals and ask what they need to execute well? How can we create some momentum with quick wins? Instead of focusing on the size of the problem, create smaller tasks and identify the "low hanging fruit" to get things moving.

Finally, I've learned to look into the mirror. I try to honestly evaluate my own delivery and determine if I'm following through on my commitments and getting results! This is a work in progress.

Wright

Mike, because of your entrepreneurial perspective and success you've been brought into associations and corporations to speak on *real-life,* down-to-earth ways to improve profitability. What practical advice can you give our readers who may be struggling to improve their bottom lines?

Foti

Profitability improvement begins with a *focus on people.* We need to "drill down" into the organization to "go up" in our profits. It's asking how can I not only influence my direct reports, but also my direct reports' people? How can I go one level lower to help and mentor someone closer to the "trench" of the business? How can I encourage and challenge them to improve results? I call it being a "CEO" (a Chief Encouragement Officer) and "CPB" (a Certified Pain in the Butt). Appreciating and encouraging their successes, but also challenging bigger and better results. Also, where can I help to remove the "barrels," the obstacles, that impede progress? I find these obstacles by asking, "What is your challenge? Where might I be of value or service?" Then I identify specific ways to deliver help.

The second key to profit improvement is to *focus on strategy.* Evaluate the current business, break it into smaller units of analysis, and look for new growth opportunities. For example, we evaluate and analyze our single product glass block business by breaking it into the varied markets we serve. We look at our margins, market share, and evaluate the resources and approaches it will take to achieve an "A" level of profitability. Then, we consider if we should fix the segment, grow it, or blow it up. We often assign responsibility by market segment to provide a more focused eye on results and a growth opportunity for new leaders.

In addition to improving the "base business," a strategy role a leader should not delegate is identifying *real-life* opportunities for the future. It's requires differentiating between what we "could do" vs. what we "should do." There are a plethora of "could do's" (different ideas that sound good during a cocktail hour), but a much smaller number of "should do's" that will produce bottom-line results. Do the in-depth analysis and then only put your money behind the "coulds."

Lastly, I look to improve profitability through a *focus on speed, efficiency, and flexibility*. What can we do to *"rev up"* the operation-improve our cash flow, increase the velocity of our inventory turns? What can we do to *"clean up"*—safe and efficient facilities, getting rid of unproductive assets that are not adding value ? Last, how can we *"limber up"* and adapt our decisions to today's reality? It's a competitive environment, so we've got to be more focused and effective than ever before!

Wright

What a great conversation on leadership today. I want to thank you for taking the time to answer my questions. I do believe the comment I was told several years ago about leadership—"If you are viewing yourself as a leader and you look behind and no one is following, then you're only out for a walk." Mike, with your approach to leadership and ability to get results through others, I believe if you look behind you, you will certainly see many people following!

Foti

Thanks David. I'm honored you would say that.

Wright

Mike, I think you're probably being a little bit too humble. People are allowing you to lead because of your knowledge, expertise and results in your industry. I really appreciate you telling us some of the things that create the trusting relationship you share with your people, which in turn generates your high level of results.

Foti

Thank you for the opportunity to contribute to this book. Leadership is definitely a journey and I'm thankful for the chance to learn and grow through the challenges and opportunities that have come my way.

Wright

Today we've been talking to Mike Foti. He is a successful entrepreneur with construction and real estate businesses located from the East Coast to the Rockies. He has increased sales of these operations 330% over the last ten years, and as we've found out today there are probably very good reasons for this—his ability to impact the bottom line and to grow leaders. Thanks again Mike.

Mike Foti is the Chief Executive Officer of Cleveland Glass Block, a construction and distribution business, which has 7 offices in 4 states. His company is a NorthCoast 99 winner for best employers and a Community Pillar Winner for community service. Through his company Leadership Builders Mike also speaks, writes, and consults on how to get results through effective leadership.

Mike Foti
Leadership Builders
1223 East 222nd Street
Euclid, Ohio 44117
Phone: 216.531.6085
Fax: 216.531.2388
Email: mfoti@leadershipbuilders.com
www.leadershipbuilders.com

Chapter 4

JOE MARK

THE INTERVIEW

David E. Wright (Wright)
Today we are talking to Joe Mark. Joe delivers profitable, highly productive business-building value to his clients using *proven* innovative leadership principles and practices. With 24 years experience as a health care executive and leadership consultant, Joe notes, "I was a successful health care executive for the first 11 years of my career. Thanks to four successive breakthrough gifts I received, I became a powerful, exceptionally successful leader and leadership coach of others." Joe's breakthrough gifts led him to develop Heart-Centered Leadership. Heart-Centered Leadership is built on a foundation of Ten Principles. He offers business leaders *proven* Practices for applying these Ten Principles that are tools for creating unsurpassed staff retention, customer satisfaction and operating profits. Joe brings this opportunity to leadership teams in the following ways: inspiring keynote addresses and break out sessions, leadership development workshops, and leadership coaching services. Mr. Mark, welcome to *Conversations on Leadership*.

Joe Mark (Mark)
Thanks, David. It's great to be with you this morning.

Wright

Joe, what led you to create Break-Through, LLC., as a professional speaking, workshop facilitation and consulting company dedicated to innovative leadership development?

Mark

The short answer to your question, David, is that I formed Break-Through, LLC to assist business leaders with practical tools for creating exceptionally profitable businesses by retaining outstanding associates who love working there and WOWing their customers. Here's the longer answer as to what I know it is going to take for businesses to realize these wonderful outcomes. Twenty years of working in medical centers ranging in complexity from $2 million in annual operating income and a couple hundred employees to $300 million in annual operating income with thousands of employees, taught me a lot about what associates are most concerned about with their leaders. As I facilitated town hall meetings, team meetings and breakfast discussions, I heard the same themes echoed time and time again. The common themes I heard from associates when I sat there and *really listened to them speak from their hearts* were,

- "Value me and my contributions. See my gifts. Appreciate them."

- "See me when you are walking in the hallway. So many times, Mr. Mark, when we are walking the corridors and a Vice President or Department Head comes by, he doesn't acknowledge us, but when he sees a Manager or Director or another Vice President, he greets him with great eye contact. I'm not invisible. See me."

- "Respect me. Respect the fact that I can handle the full truth. Share financial statements. Share market share information about how we are doing. Share how we're doing with our customers. Give us the good news *and* the bad news."

- "Include me. I'm on the firing line. I'm out there with patients, with physicians and with families every day. I know how to improve service and so do my teammates. We want to be more involved. Our team wants to be more involved. Include us. We want to own our schedule, our staffing plans, our quality program. We want to interview new team members that come into the team."

- "Be clear with your expectations. So many times, the only time we hear from a supervisor is when things are wrong. We need to know what is expected from us and how our performance will be evaluated."

I call these recurring associate themes, *The Common Voice of Frustration*, David. Legions of associates are working in all manner of businesses who aren't contributing their very best *because their leaders haven't created a culture conducive to getting it.* Before they will give their absolute best, they must be safe, trusted, respected and recognized for their gifts.

What's missing is associates are not bringing their hearts into the places where they work because they simply *aren't* safe and valued. They check their hearts at the door and they pick them up when they leave work at the end of the day. They take them to the Boy Scouts, the Girl Scouts and to the nursing home for volunteer service. They take their full passion and energies, and gifts and they share them *where they know they are valued and where it is safe to share them.* We simply aren't getting their best in most work places because we (their leaders) haven't earned their best. We aren't getting their best because the stress they feel from *not* being seen, heard, respected and valued is taking a huge toll on their health.

What we're seeing in America, across business, education, government and agency sectors is a very disturbing decline in our health. We lead the world in chronic disease and our employees are right in the thick of this trend. This results in excessive absenteeism, sub par productivity and eventually high, incredibly expensive turnover that is disruptive for teams and a huge blow to the bottom line. This is a completely unacceptable and avoidable cost of doing business! *There is an alternative!*

Dissatisfied customers are sick and tired of receiving less than acceptable, let alone exceptional value. This should come as no surprise when the associates serving them and producing things for them don't feel seen, respected, heard or trusted. How could it be any other way?

The *alternative*, David, is *Heart-Centered Leadership* and my passion is in bringing its Principles and proven business Practices to leadership teams who are committed to creating Heart-Centered Organizations where *everyone* is respected, valued, heard, seen and trusted. These are the 21st Century organizations that will be leading the way in creating gold standard results in associate retention, WOWED customers and operating income. *Everyone has a Heart-Centered Leader within, David.* I am committed to bringing what I have developed and market tested with great success to the leaders of our business, education, government and agency organizations who want more...who must have more and will be relentless until they get it.

Wright

I recognize myself in some of your examples from different times in my life, especially in my search for self-actualization. In your company material, you refer to your mission "to assist others as an inspired guide in awakening to and claiming their greatness to create a more loving and peaceful world." What does that mean for you and for your clients, Joe?

Mark

David, for me and for my clients, it means seeking out and receiving the assistance we need in awakening to and claiming our Life Purpose and Passions—and when we do, what a peace-filled and loving world we will enjoy! By Life Purpose, I mean what I am here to become and do. By Passions, I mean what gets you to jump out of bed in the morning and want to run to work. What energizes you? What makes you happiest in life? *When we bring that energy into the workplace, we are going to see some truly amazing things in terms of retaining outstanding associates, WOWING customers and producing exceptional bottom lines.*

This is about our standing fully in our power and supporting each other in doing the same. It comes from an underlying belief that we live in an *abundant* world, that there's plenty for everyone and it's time for individuals to create peace and prosperity.

Wright

The central or underlying theme in your leadership keynotes, workshops, and consulting services is the "Heart Centered Leader." What are the characteristics of a Heart- Centered leader? How will I know I am in the presence of one?

Mark

I *know* that I am standing in the presence of a Heart-Centered Leader when I see him *practicing* the Principles of such a leader. Talk is (definitely!) cheap, David, when it comes to a leader's establishing credibility in an organization. It is action that counts. Here is what I see Heart-Centered Leaders doing as principled practitioners...

First and foremost, he is a person of *Integrity* as he honors his commitments and speaks truthfully. He does what he says he is going to do. He shows up on time. His voice, body and tone are congruent with his words.

Second, he holds himself and others *Accountable*. He practices tough love by holding himself and others accountable to their commitments. He teaches that selling each other short in not honoring our commitments is an unacceptable price *all* end up paying for many times over.

Third, he is *Compassionate*. He leads *from his heart* knowing that his head is always there to do what it does well. He acknowledges feelings. He honors feelings expecting that they be managed responsibly.

Fourth, he is *Inspirational!* He inspires follower-ship with his high-energy presence, focused, delivered intentions and passionate purpose. He devotes time and other resources to what he is passionate about and he delegates, dumps or shares what he is dispassionate about. He *knows* Who He Is and radiates it!

Fifth, he is *Accepting*. He accepts people simply for *Who They Are*. He is non-judgmental, choosing to accept *what is* versus labeling it right or wrong. He honors diversity and the unique gifts that people bring to the organization versus attempting to hire and make others like him.

Sixth, he is *Appreciative*. He let's me know, *right now*, how he appreciates my contribution and *the difference* it just made for the customer or co-worker. He knows what *I find meaningful* in the way of recognition for a job well done. He *publicly shares* how much he appreciates my gifts to the organization *and* me.

Seventh, he is *Intimate* in sharing W*ho He Is* and he knows the power of sharing his vulnerability and his humanity with others in the organization. He stands powerfully tall in expressing his humanity in his work and non-work life. In doing so, others are literally freed to mirror what is Intimately Them.

Eighth, he is wonderfully *Present*! *Nothing* distracts him from his singular focus on what I am sharing with him. I feel valued, heard, seen and respected by his mostly silent, occasionally nodding presence with me. He freely gives me his time when I know he has many pressing responsibilities and demands on his time. In this moment, I *am* the most important person in his world.

Ninth, he exudes a great sense of *Humor*. He laughs at his shortcomings instead of taking himself too seriously. He knows the healing power of humor and masterfully shares his when the team or someone on the team is most in need of a laugh. He chooses to remain happy in spite of whatever is whirling all around him.

Last and definitely not least, David, he is *Forgiving*. He shows that there is no failure, only learning and improving, by taking a situation that doesn't go well and uses it as a teachable moment. He teaches and models that forgiveness is first and foremost *for the forgiver*—that it clears out the darkness of hate, revenge, betrayal and hurt and replaces it with light.

Wright

Who are your customers and what benefits can they realize in adopting Heart Centered Leadership?

Mark

When I first started putting the Heart Centered Leadership Principles, Practices and development tools together, David, I focused *exclusively* on executive and mid-level leader development in business, education, government and agency organizations. These are the folks that make or break any major culture enhancement initiative in an organization. *If Heart-Centered Leadership is going to be embraced in an organization, it is imperative that the CEO and her team be fully bought into the Principles and Practices before introducing it beyond them.*

I strongly recommend meeting first with the CEO and then with the CEO and her team to introduce them to Heart-Centered Leadership, what it has to offer organizations and the commitments needed on their part to create a Heart-Centered Organization.

The best way to do this is to begin by giving them an inspirational talk on the power of Heart-Centered Leadership so that the executive team can learn the Principles, Practices and tools for creating such an organization. If I get a "Thanks but no thanks" response, we simply part company, wishing each other well.

If I get a "WOW, this is incredibly exciting and holds a lot of promise for our organization—where do we go next?" response, then I suggest that the executive team commit to participating in a workshop with me to immerse themselves more in Heart-Centered Leadership to get a clear picture and experience with it before going any further organizationally.

At the end of the workshop, we process the experience together and I leave with the understanding that the CEO will get back with me with her decision to go to the next step or to bid each other farewell. At that point, there is minimal resource commitment expended for exploring the opportunity. *It is the next step that calls for full CEO and executive team commitment.*

This step involves a series of inspirational presentations that I would make to all members of the organization, kicked off by the CEO informing all that I am speaking with them to introduce Heart-Centered Leadership and the expected return on investment in incorporating it as a major culture enhancement initiative. She would express her and the executive team's commitment to Heart-Centered Leadership based on her experience in the executive team workshop and her *knowing* that it will yield the desired returns when fully embraced by the organization. It would be made clear by the CEO that she trusts that there is a *Heart-Centered Leader in everyone* working in the organization and that it is up to her and her team to model and teach its Principles and Practices.

Wright

Can you really assist executives and mid-level managers in transforming into Heart-Centered Leaders? I mean, can you really "teach old dogs new tricks?"

Mark

Absolutely! I can provide the guidance, the developmental workshops, and the coaching for leaders. Their answers and how they answer some questions I have for them before I decide to work with them (and vice versa) will tell me a lot about their *understanding* of Heart-Centered Leadership, what is has to offer and the *commitments* they will need to honor to go further in their development with it. I ask, "Do you have an openness to learn? Are you *really* ready to go to school, to be students again? Are you willing to be led as well as to lead? What are your reservations with proceeding?" We talk about What's at Risk to go forward together and What's at Risk if we don't.

Wright

You know CEOs today face short term, bottom line, what have you done for us lately pressure. And you've walked in a CEO's shoes. How do you go about convincing a CEO to invest in developing Heart-Centered Leaders that holds more mid or long term return in face of the near term pressures?

Mark

That's a great question, David. Those near term pressures are very real. I have walked in a CEO's shoes and that's something that I have that's valuably unique as an inspirational speaker and work-shop facilitator. I have taken theory and principle and *incorporated them successfully in the business world of practice*. I would first say to a CEO, "My job *isn't* to convince you. My job, my mission, *is* to offer you services and tools that will significantly improve your short, near, and long-term business outcomes. I can offer you concrete, hands on, face to face *opportunities* for materially improving your bottom line, for helping you keep the absolute best employees and for WOWING your customers." My commitment to them is that within three months, they will realize breakthroughs in these three business out-comes *if* there is a genuine buy-in by the CEO and executive team in learning and immediately applying what they learn in the workshop and individual coaching sessions. They have to be willing to go to school as I mentioned a few minutes ago in terms of learning new things about themselves and about Heart-Centered Leadership. The litmus test question I ask them about proceeding forward together is this: *"If this sounds a little scary and too risky for you, how is what you're doing today working for you?"* I listen to how they are doing in keeping their best employees, in WOWING their customers and in improving their bottom line. Typically what I get back is, "What we are doing isn't working so great for us. Tell us some more, Joe."

Wright

When you are asked for examples of Heart Centered Leader role models, who do you suggest and what are you basing your recommen-dations on?

Mark

I answer that several ways, David. In terms of the famous, I like to name some Masters of Heart-Centered Leadership that influenced me and my developing Heart-Centered Leadership: Mother Teresa of

Calcutta, Mahatma Gandhi, Jesus of Nazareth, Abraham Lincoln, former president Jimmy Carter. These people are exemplars of *all ten* Heart Centered Leadership Principles *in practice*. I then share examples of powerful people who stepped up in my life and made a huge difference in influencing me as a developing leader and what they modeled for me in living one or more of the Principles. I end by asking the person to reflect on the Heart-Centered leaders in his life, past and present, who stepped up for him. "Who exhibited Heart-Centered mastery for you on one or more of the Principles that helped you develop those attributes?"

Wright

Let's go back to one of the Heart-Centered Leader attributes that you mentioned earlier—*vulnerability*, risking being *intimate* in front of one's subordinates. Isn't it risky, particularly for a CEO to appear vulnerable?

Mark

I expect that most CEOs have some fear about "appearing vulnerable." Their fear sounds something like this—"Oh my God, Joe, if I do that, I'll be ruined—no more credibility, no more being in control, no more respect from my team or Board!" I ask him to imagine the scene—what it would look like, sound like and feel like in sharing his heart and soul, "open kimono" so to speak, in his full humanity...and end *WONDERFULLY!* What I get mostly in reply is, "How could my making myself vulnerable in front of my direct reports or management team possibly end up *WONDERFULLY?*" Most will struggle horribly to imagine, even for a moment, how there could possibly be a good outcome to such a display of "weakness." Inevitably, I will be challenged, "You were a CEO, Joe, how can you even suggest that there would be a WONDERFUL outcome in being vulnerable with my team?"

My experience has been that when I risk sharing Joe fully and without pretense, the return comes back to me a thousand fold. Others feel freer to be fully themselves. I explain to the executive that it is this intimacy that brings us to our oneness. It accentuates in real ways that we are all healing from our own wounds and we don't have to do it alone anymore. We don't have to wear what I call the "okay" mask that we all tend to wear around. We know that we are leaders *as* flesh and blood brothers and sisters.

Wright

Could you share a story from your executive career that illustrates how you stood in your vulnerability as a Heart Centered Leader and what happened?

Mark

Sure. This was the most powerful epiphany experience I have had in my life. It took place in a hospital auditorium full of frightened, angry managers, department heads and vice presidents as I was being introduced to them as their interim COO. To give you a sense of the situation, David, this loyal group of leaders were facing their *fourth* due diligence review by a prospective purchaser in less than one year and an interim, contracted executive group had been brought in three months prior to my arrival to work with them to accomplish two feats—stem the flow of red ink and position the medical center for sale.

My charge was to rally the troops behind a vision of what a revitalized medical center would look like with new owners infusing much needed capital into facilities and equipment so it could effectively compete with the other medical centers in the area. *Translation*—keep morale up. Keep the management team focused on the task at hand. Stop the financial hemorrhage. Keep the key admitting physicians and surgeons to stabilize inpatient volumes. Last but not least, convince the members of the management team, who are thinking about leaving, to stick it out to help lead a revitalized medical center to new prosperity.

Standing in front of these people, I am on a stage platform under hot lights looking up and out into a fairly dark auditorium at approximately 150 middle managers, senior managers, and first line supervisors. As I am about to introduce myself and roll out the plan for meeting our two objectives, tears swelled up in my eyes. I'm thinking, "Oh my God, what's going on here?" What I realized *in a flash* was I was feeling their pain and it slammed right into mine from having recently separated from my wife of 23 years and very much missing my two kids. In my loss for words and with tears rolling down my eyes, I said a silent prayer asking Spirit for help. I heard a thought in my head that lovingly said, "Trust them, be fully Joe. You are here to heal one another." I looked up to them as the were holding this incredibly respectful and present silence, David, and as I was composing myself, I heard this incredible explosion of applause followed by a voice that said, "It's OK Joe, we are with you!" I shared with them who Joe Mark is and my passion for working with them to keep our medical center in business. I was born in that medical center, as were my brothers and sisters, my dad passed over from it nine years ago, the medical center is in my home town and is serving thousands who would otherwise find it difficult accessing quality, timely care—this is my medical center, too! They got it. I got it.

In that moment, I knew what it meant to be a Heart-Centered Leader standing vulnerably in front of a group and trusting that they would respect my humanity. The gift they received from me in doing so was the freedom to be fully human themselves in this very trying time. This freeing trust drew us together and we moved a mountain.

Wright

Goodness, inspiration before perspiration, is that it?

Mark

Absolutely, what it boils down to is capture their hearts. Nurture them by leading as a Heart-Centered Leader and they will walk over hot coals with you in tough times and share the bounty with you in the good times. They will do it because they *know* it's about everybody winning. Customers win, suppliers win and they certainly win as a working team *in community* with each other.

Wright

Breakthrough differences made in organizations—you assert in your material that they flow from followers who are inspired by their leaders. What has your experience taught you about this?

Mark

Well, David, it has taught me that so many of us in business, business leaders, continue to miss a huge piece. We believe that we will discover terrific breakthroughs and we'll keep thriving by promoting *more head work*—more data crunching and analysis, more "working smarter," which, to me, is one of the biggest euphemisms in the business world. It really means working harder with less. Head work is important, don't misunderstand me; however, it's been proven time and time again that it's *not anywhere near enough! The missing piece is Heart Centered Leadership*—inviting followers into the power of Who They Are, what they feel, and creating with them an organization known for genuinely caring for everyone associated with it. It is about inspired Heart-Centered Leaders igniting the heart-fire in their followers that creates "The Whoosh!" You get breakthrough after breakthrough after breakthrough resulting in gold standard staff retention, WOWED customers and operating margins. Empowered, valued, respected and joyful staff do the customer WOWING that creates the exceptional operating income and opportunity for corporate tithing.

In summary, Heart leads supported by head, and I believe we've had it the other way around or, in far too many places, Heart is kept out of it—reserved for other aspects of our lives outside of work. What comes when Heart partners with knowledge is Wisdom and Compassion. The best summary of Heart-Centered Leadership is this—when Wisdom and Compassion "marry" knowledge, truly amazing business results happen.

Wright

The Heart Centered Leader—who is really looking for this kind of leadership in the marketplace and why, if you will?

Mark

That's a really challenging question and I answer it this way. I'd say multiple groups yearn for this kind of leadership. We have to go back to *who wins*, David. Leaders win. Followers win. Suppliers win. Customers win. Shareholders win. Ultimately, community members win because they have a healthy business supporting their community in so many ways.

There *are* Heart-Centered Leaders leading organizations today. My contention, David, is that they are few and far between. We need many more. We need *legions* of leaders championing the Ten Principles of Heart-Centered Leadership and applying them in the marketplace.

Followers are out there in the millions and they will literally run to and compete for the opportunity to join an organization that lives Heart Centered Leadership! Organizational leaders who get this will be the standard bearers for their industry sector. *Imagine* the turnover cost savings when this happens in a big way—when people love their organization and invite their friends and colleagues to come join the team! They'll be calling the best of the best out there saying, "David, Joe, you have to come check this out. This is absolutely the best place to work in America. They respect our gifts and our energies here. We're *all* in here making it happen together, and you know what? I've worked in places like yours where we basically ragged on the bosses through e-mail, coffee and water cooler jam sessions and restroom complaint stops. So much of our time was wasted feeling worthless and complaining. That doesn't happen in *this* place!"

Imagine suppliers who are treated as valued, long-term partners in a win-win business relationship. No more milking the last nickel and dime concession out of these partners. It's about them working *with us* to find more effective, efficient ways to run our business. This really boils down, David, to developing a *knowing* that we are part of an abundant universe, that there really is more than enough to meet everyone's needs, suppliers as well as we purchasers.

Customers come out the biggest winners as they are WOWED by the value we continue creating with them. Customers of a Heart-Centered Organization know that they are *THE* integral part of it— without them, there is no business! When they get heart caring, when they get anticipation of their needs, when we exceed their wildest expectations, we get customers for life. I've had family members write me as the CEO after they had a loved one pass over in the medical center saying things like, "Your staff was so sensitive. They sat with us when I know they had a lot of other pressing patient demands. From the time our dad hit your door in admitting to the time he passed on, we always felt loved in the place." I kept their letters in a box, David, and I sent congratulatory letters to the teams for a great heart-felt job well done. We often would get letters to the editor in the local newspaper acknowledging that the medical center was so much more than a high technology place of curing—that it was an exceptional place where people *really* care. That's the bottom line difference of a Heart-Centered Organization.

Wright

You speak of collaboration being key for business-to-business and interpersonal relationships in the new millennium. Why, particularly when so much energy and resources are being poured into zero sum competition?

Mark

Yes, collaboration is key. In fact, I would say it will prove *vital* for business organizations to thrive in the new millennium—those who are committed to attracting and keeping the best staff, WOWING customers and generating remarkable operating margins. Zero sum competition is founded on a premise of lack—that there is a finite amount of anything in the Universe and that in order for me to have a share in it, I have to compete with you to get it. Zero sum competition, in a nutshell, means in order for me to win, you have to lose. So if one is the sum total and I have one, you have to have zero. The bottom line is someone wins at the expense of another losing.

Collaboration is founded on the premise of abundance—that together, we can all have what we need and more. I would challenge advocates of zero sum competition this way—"How has zero sum competition served you, your associates, your suppliers, your customers and your community?" My knowing from serving as a CEO who competed with other CEOs for market share is that it didn't serve any constituency group well. We *rarely* explored opportunities to collaborate for the greater good. We were expected by our boards and the owners of our systems to take market share from the other guy. You get what you expect. We can do far better with collaboration. We can all win.

Wright

I hear how you see zero sum v. collaborative relationships work externally in the marketplace, Joe, how do you see them working internally—inside an organization?

Mark

Zero sum competition within an organization is sheer lunacy! Heart-Centered Leaders know that the key to creating Heart-Centered Organizations is this—Everyone Wins! Heart-Centered Leaders are "silo busters." Our job is to *shatter the* silos that keep people looking up and down but never across. Heart-Centered Leaders hold people accountable for how their decisions affect people to their left, to their right, on the floor above them and on the floor below them. My experience taught me, David, that internal, zero sum, I have to win at your expense, comes from a culturally laden belief in scarcity that has to go! It kills innovation, responsible risk taking, cooperation, trust and productivity. It leads to data hoarding, division, sabotage and subterfuge. The real driver behind all of it is fear. I love the definition of fear, and I don't know where I picked this up, but it's perfect. F.E.A.R is False Evidence Appearing Real. It literally just sucks the life force right out of people in an organization, and we need to help people face their fear and move through them. My bias, and I'm probably going to crunch a number of toes with some readers saying this, is that too many of us in American business, David, have bought into what I call business Darwinism—survival of the fittest.

This is bad enough between competing entities; it's basically a shameless travesty inside organizations that foster it. I think until we redefine, David, from our hearts what success is and how it's to be achieved together, we're doomed to more of the same-old, same-old that I can only succeed at your expense or your loss.

I know there is a healthy, profitable, people-building alternative to great business and great living. It is Heart-Centered Leadership and its sound enculturation into business organizations is my passion.

Wright

Do you see graduate business schools such as MBA programs developing curriculums including courses on Heart-Centered Leadership Principles and Practices, and if so, what would you recommend regarding the backgrounds of faculty to teach them?

Mark

I'd love to see that happen, David. I'd love to see our graduate business school deans recruit experienced, adjunct, Heart Centered Leader faculty from their business communities to teach the Ten Principles and Practices of Heart-Centered Leadership to graduate students. This introductory course would include case studies featuring business stories that illustrate the power of each Principle applied in a business, noting what differences it made to associates, suppliers, customers, the bottom line and the community.

Other courses could be shaped as experiential workshops focused on specific leadership skill development. Graduate students would sit in both leader and follower seats of learning to *experience* being on the giving and receiving end of this leadership. Each workshop would focus on a specific Heart-Centered Leadership Principle—its attributes, tools for applying the Principle in practice and the pay-offs the applications will yield when well executed in the workplace.

Imagine these graduate students, David, coming out with powerfully effective leadership skill sets as well as with management skill sets. Our universities do a great job teaching quantitative methods, quality improvement, organizational theory and practice, marketing, business law and other management type offerings. The real challenge today, as I see it, is that we have to teach them how to lead people well, *from their hearts,* backed by all the great head tools that we teach them about managing things.

Wright

Well, Joe, let me ask you. Are you up for some inspirational dreaming with me?

Mark

Sure!

Wright

Let's look about 10 years from now on the world where organizational leaders have embraced Heart-Centered Leadership. How is that world different from the one we live in now?

Mark

Heart-Centered Leadership has fundamentally changed our world. People are living *purposely*. They are passionate in fulfilling their life purpose and in supporting their neighbors and co-workers in doing the same. People are happy! Newspaper articles have shifted from gore, violence and what's wrong with the world to amazing things that are happening in local school systems, in the local tire factory, in the local medical center.

Amazing breakthroughs are happening in medicine, business, government and education, as businesses in these sectors are led by experienced, Heart-Centered Leaders committed to everyone benefiting from their collaborative work. These breakthroughs have led to the creation of new businesses offering well-paying jobs and great benefits to those hired into them.

Businesses are enjoying incredibly high associate retention. Associates are choosing to work in them because they are valued, respected, heard, seen and offered development opportunities as a matter of course. They love being part of an organization that is built on Heart-Centered Leadership Principles and Practices.

Collaborative business-supplier company partnerships are flourishing, built on win-win long-term contracts resulting in powerful, synergistic business opportunities for both. WOWED customers are the norm across business sectors. When I approach "Company A" with my business, I know that I am going to receive great value for my dollar! I know that I am going to be treated by their associates exactly the way they want to be treated when they come to my business for service. This experience is normative across business and industry lines. Where it isn't normative, its leaders make it so or it goes out of business. Businesses are experiencing outstanding profitability and they are tithing a percentage of their operating incomes to local charitable organizations in the communities where the business is generated. Communities are flourishing in a period of abundance realization, empowerment and exceptional service. Nations are enjoying peace and interdependent abundance creation as we have learned to make the most of our unique gifts and treasures. We have mastered fear and are champions of Accountability, Integrity, Compassion, Inspiration, Acceptance, Appreciation, Humor, Presence, Intimacy and Forgiveness.

I'll close my response with a story, David. I shared one epiphany wake-up experience earlier in our interview. This is another one and I share it because it illustrates the commitment of what it will take for this vision that is 10 years out becoming a reality.

A Sister (nun) CEO I worked with a number of years ago shared this with me— "Joe, you have a great head, you are a powerful strategic thinker and you are masterful in managing projects, budgets and processes. You get very good results. To become a great Leader and get great results, master this: It is all about relationships, relationships, relationships." David, when she first hit me with that, it just didn't connect. It wasn't an immediate epiphany experience, in fact, I was really insulted because I saw myself as a pretty powerful leader who had accomplished a lot in his first 11 years in the business. As Spirit provides, I was gifted with a series of opportunities over the course of the next six years or so that led me into to my heart and into developing Heart Centered Leadership. In each of those experiences, I kept hearing Sister's voice, "Joe, it's relationships, relationships, relationships!" I got what she meant and I had the opportunity to apply my new learning as an executive in some very challenging situations. I evolved into a Heart-Centered Leader by committing to living as wide awake in Now as possible and in choosing to see and experience the best in life. Heart-Centered Leadership evolved from this commitment as I witnessed its power in the workplace in creating gold-standard retention, WOWED customers and operating margins. "Old dogs *can* learn new tricks," David. This one did and I am very much looking forward to sharing Heart-Centered Leadership with others to help them significantly cut their learning curve to get what they must have in their organizations and in their lives.

Wright

Joe, I tell you I have spent too many years of my life in corporations wondering what in the world my leader and my management team were up to, and this sounds to me to be a great, great leadership approach. I can't wait. I know you are working on a book. I can't wait. I'm going to be standing in line at my friendly Barnes & Noble to get your Heart-Centered Leadership book. I really can't wait until it comes out, and I want you to know how much I appreciate your being with us today on *Conversations on Leadership*. Thank you so much for your time.

Mark

Well, thank you, David, and thanks for the opportunity to be able to talk with you about Heart-Centered Leadership.

Wright

Today we have been talking to Joe Mark. He is a successful business executive. He comes with 24 years experience as a health care executive and leadership consultant and, as we have found out today, knows a lot about leadership. And I suggest that when he gets his book out, you join me in that line. Thank you, Joe.

Mark

Thank you, David.

About The Author

Joe's inspirational and informative speeches, workshops and consultative services are designed to prepare business, government, education and agency leaders for creating Heart-Centered Organizations that create *exceptional productivity and profit, staff retention and customer satisfaction results*. From his 20 years of executive and consulting experience as an inspirational leader, Joe has learned the power of Heart-Centered Leadership in breaking through the barriers that separate the interests of leaders and followers. Joe provides *proven* "tools" business leaders can immediately utilize to incorporate the *10 Principles and Practices of Heart-Centered Leadership* into their organizations. Many consultant-speakers *talk theoretically* about business principles and practices. *Joe shares what works* from what he has successfully implemented as a former VP, EVP and President in six organizations. Look into the *experiential difference* Joe can bring to your organization through his page at www.bookaspeaker.com.

Joe Mark
Email: jmark@voyager.net

Chapter 5

DR. RAY RUSSELL

David E. Wright (Wright)

Today we are talking to Dr. Ray Russell. He is the author of the award winning book, *The Miracle of Personal Leadership*, which contains the skills essential for success in the 21st Century, but not commonly taught in the educational system. As a leadership coach, his mission is to: "raise people and organizations to their highest value." Ray has been president and board member of more than two dozen corporate, civic, and professional organizations such as director of the Hills National Management Center at Kansas State University. He was the president and executive director of the American Animal Hospital Association and president of Employee America SW, Inc. Dr. Ray Russell has earned three degrees studying at the Ohio State University, Arizona State University, University of Phoenix, and Kansas State University where he was an All-American Hurdler on the Track Team. He has received numerous honors and awards for his contributions to his community, state, and nation such as Mesa Arizona Citizen of the Year, Arizona Jaycees Outstanding Young Man and was selected as the University of Phoenix Alumni of the Year for 2002. Dr. Russell, welcome to *Conversations on Leadership*.

Dr. Ray Russell (Russell)
Thank you.

Wright
Dr. Russell, why do you say leaders are on the endangered species list?

Russell
They are an endangered species because leaders are so rare today. We talk a lot about leadership, but most people really don't understand it. They confuse leadership and management. In today's world, we really need more leaders who will take action and get a job done. Nearly everyone needs more knowledge and information on how to apply leadership skills.

Wright
Why did you write the book, *The Miracle of Personal Leadership*? I understand it was selected as one of the top three books published in the self-help and professional categories by The Midwest Independent Publishers Association.

Russell
I've had a passion for leadership for many years. This fire was ignited in me while I was serving as the course director of weeklong leadership development courses for volunteer Boy Scout Leaders. I observed life changing behaviors in the participants of these courses. Teachers became better teachers, parents improved their parenting skills and business leaders were more effective leaders in their professions. For example, one medical doctor doubled his income in six months, by applying these leadership skills in his medical practice. I was so impressed with the results I observed; I believed that everyone would benefit from this training. This leadership development course was 20 years ahead of the times. As a member of the National Speakers Association, leadership has become a very popular subject for speakers. I discovered Personal Leadership was the missing ingredient in Organizational Leadership. This happened to me when I ran for the United States Congress against John McCain, when he was first elected. I got in the race very late and was defeated by just a few votes. Being deeply in debt after this political campaign, I did a lot of studying, thinking, and planning. I started interviewing people that had gone through difficult times in their lives. After interviewing

nearly 200 people who had overcome serious challenges in their lives, I discovered what I called "Personal Leadership." I observed that these people were able to lead themselves through some very serious obstacles. This led me to discover there's a difference between organizational leadership and what I called personal leadership. This is what got me started on writing *The Miracle of Personal Leadership.* I believe, if you can't lead yourself, how can you lead anyone else? Personal Leadership is the missing ingredient in Organizational Leadership. It is the foundation for all leadership.

Wright

What is the personal leadership model that you describe in your book? Does it really work with the people who apply it?

Russell

Absolutely, the Personal Leadership Model is powerful. The night of the election was my final night of class for my master's degree in business management at the University of Phoenix. When I started writing my leadership book, the focus was on business, but it became apparent that everybody needed Personal Leadership skills. I developed my Personal Leadership model after interviewing nearly 200 people. This model consists of five major points: (1) **Painting a picture in your mind.** This is your personal purpose or mission statement. (2) **Develop a personal written strategy.** This strategy is your personal business plan. Write down seven or eight things you want with three or four action steps under each objective. (3) **Develop personal energy.** Energy is life. Everyone would be more successful if they had more energy. (4) **Personal Empowerment.** You empower yourself by loving what you do. I lost the election to John McCain because I really wasn't committed and John McCain was. If I ever fail to get results, it is usually the result of poor commitment. Two other empowering skills that everyone needs today are performance empowerment and interactive empowerment. A lot of people have one of these, but not both. Performance empowerment is the ability to get a job done. Interactive empowerment is how you relate with people. Both of these skills are essential today. Some people relate well but don't get things done and others get a job done, but don't relate well with others. Some people talk about empowering other people. You don't empower others—you empower yourself. (5) **Setting an example or modeling leadership** is the final part of this model. The example you set is the heart of leadership. Some people say that the best leader is simply the person who scts the highest example. These five points make up the Personal Leadership Model. I could tell you hundreds of stories of how application of this model has helped people overcome obstacles in their life and achieve results they may not have dreamed were possible.

Wright

As a member of the National Speakers Association, you give keynote addresses and workshops on leadership, but what does your talk entitled, *Treat Yourself Like a Business,* mean? How does a person treat themselves like a business?

Russell

A large number of new start-up businesses go out of business in the very first year for one reason or another. The few that survive, within five years 85 percent to 95 percent of those are gone. One of the reasons many of these businesses have problems is that the manager tends to treat their business more like a hobby instead of like a business. People have the same tendency. We could all achieve better results if we would learn to treat ourselves more like a business rather than like a hobby. By following my Personal Leadership Model, we can treat ourselves more like a business. This will enable us to improve our performance and achieve outstanding results.

As I go back through the Personal Leadership Model, think of yourself as a business. For example, (1) Paint a picture in your mind. That is your purpose statement or personal mission statement. If a business doesn't have a vision or mission statement, or if they don't follow it, they are going to have problems. In fact as a consultant, I saw a lot of businesses go out of business or have financial trouble because they didn't have a mission statement or they didn't follow it. I say the same is true with us. If we don't have one or if we don't follow it, it will effect our performance. My personal purpose or mission statement is to "Raise people and organizations to their highest value." This means me and my family or if I am teaching, my students. As a consultant it is the organization and the people in that business. The personal picture you paint in your mind is very important, just like a mission statement is to a business. (2) The next step is to develop a personal written strategy. This is your personal business plan. A business may go out of business, or at least may not achieve the results they could, because they either don't have a business plan or they don't follow it. The same is true with us. I have always set goals, but the first year I did this I was practicing veterinary medicine. I took one sheet of paper and I wrote down things I wanted, financially, intellectually, physically and spiritually, etc. Then I wrote down three or four action steps under each one. I spent at least 16 hours developing my personal strategy or business plan. I recommend that you spend at least eight hours developing your personal strategy on one sheet of paper. Look at this plan every day. The first year I did this I doubled my income and reduced the hours I worked by 30 to 35 hours a week. I was so impressed with the power of doing this, I've done it almost every year since. Now, as I said, I've set goals before but this seemed to work more effectively for me and that was my personal business plan which I called my personal written strategy. (3) The next part of the model is to energize yourself. There was a study of a thousand fast growing businesses in the United States and Canada. This study revealed that a high level of energy was the common factor responsible for the growth of these businesses. These were large and small businesses. If energy is that important to a business, then why isn't it important to us? Energy comes from the people in a business. Each one of us could be far more successful in our lives if we would develop more energy. (4) The next part of the Personal Leadership Model is Personal Empowerment. One of the biggest problems in business today, is poor people-skills. In fact, I like to call our time on earth today as the "Age of Relationships." A lot of leaders in businesses are having difficulties because they don't have adequate interpersonal skills. Interpersonal and performance skills are essential to run a successful business. If you treat yourself like a business, you will get a job done and get along with people. (5) The last part of the model is setting an example or modeling leadership. We could call this the heart of leadership. It is generally recognized that the best leader is simply the one who sets the highest example. Corporate values are critical to the success of any business or organization. The same is true with each of us. We must have high standards and values to be successful in our personal or professional life. Many companies believe they have high standards, but they don't live by them. Application of these principles is essential to running a successful business. These same things are important for each of us; therefore, applying the Personal Leadership Model in our lives results in us "treating ourselves more like a business."

Wright

You did a research project while you were the Director of The Hill's National Management Center at Kansas State University. What did you discover from your interviews of 200 employers you mentioned in hiring new college graduates?

Russell

My experience in running my own business, education and consulting has taught me how important good people skills are to success. When I was teaching business management at Kansas State University, I started the series of management classes by teaching people skills. My students said, "We don't want this soft people skill stuff, we want the real management." I asked, "What's the real management?" They said, "finance, planning, human resources, etc." This experience stimulated my mind because I knew how important people skills are in operating a successful business. They all thought they had good people skills, but this motivated me to do a research study of business owners who would hire new graduates. I interviewed 200 business owners and asked them what they liked and didn't like about new graduates they hired in their businesses. Almost without exception, they told me that the new students were technically well prepared, but nearly 100 percent said, they do not have the people skills to relate with our clients effectively and until they develop those skills, they cannot make me money. I went back and told my students what I had found, giving them some examples. After this the students started evaluating interpersonal skills, developing relationships, communicating and working together, as the most important thing they learned in all the business courses we taught. This study was an eye opener to me, to hear this from all these business owners. It is apparent that universities often neglect teaching these important skills. Business schools teach all kinds of business classes, but they really do not put the emphasis on human relations or interpersonal skills which is so critical to be successful with the customers and leading their staff.

Wright

What did you learn from the weeklong leadership development courses you directed for volunteer youth leaders throughout the United States and several foreign countries?

Russell

These Leadership Development courses taught the essential leadership competencies so important in improving performance and how to apply it in their work or personal lives. These competencies not only helped the participants be better volunteer leaders, but it assisted them in nearly every area of their lives. They not only became more successful in their businesses, but they also improved in their role as parents and spouses. The major thing I learned was how important leadership skills are in nearly every aspect of our lives. I observed the same positive results in many areas of the world where I had the opportunity to conduct these leadership development courses.

Wright

As a Certified Professional Behavioral/Values/Attributes and TriMetrix™ Analyst, how do you use these computerized reports on your Internet Delivery System, to select employees, develop productive teams, resolve conflicts and develop leaders?

Russell

These various behavioral/attitude/values and attribute instruments are very important tools which are helpful in employee selection, teambuilding, conflict resolution and leadership development. Using these instruments, along with training, has been very effective in increasing productivity by 20-80 percent. They are important tools in resolving conflicts, improving customer service and effectively supervising workers Completing these instruments is not a test. There are no right or wrong answers. It only takes ten minutes to complete the Managing for Success profile. The computer prints out a 26-page report to help you communicate more effectively with people who are different from you. It will identify your greatest value to an organization along with your ideal work environment, how to motivate, how to manage, and areas for improvement. The next step involves a personal coaching session where we go over their report line by line. This is followed with a training session involving the whole team to help team members understand themselves and identify their strengths and weaknesses. Diversity brings strength to a team if we understand and appreciate it—otherwise conflict may result. One of the major problems today is that people don't understand people who have different behavioral styles. They tend to think if they are different, something is wrong with them. These reports along with coaching and training is very effective in helping people to understand each other better. Attitudes and values profiles are also important to add to this understanding, because this helps people understand why people do what they do. These instruments are great tools in employee selection, building strong work teams, conflict resolution, improving supervision and in leadership development. While I was serving as president of an employment company, we used these instruments in employee selection. These tools helped us in selection of 1000 employees for a major corporation. They were having a 50 percent attrition in these positions. We were able to reduce this attrition from 50 percent down to 7 percent by using these tools in the employee selection process.

Wright

That's great.

Russell

I have used thousands of these instruments over the past 20 years. The results have been very beneficial because research shows the most effective people are those who understand the most about themselves and others. With this knowledge, they can appreciate their differences, which is essential to improving relationships.

Wright

I have been taking the D.I.S.C at least a couple times a year since 1973. It is incredible how accurate they are.

Russell

These reports are validated at 89 to 95 percent accurate. They are just tools, but when used properly, they can be a valuable instrument in selection and development of people. Since I now have them available on the internet, I have some companies who would not even think of hiring a person without first running these reports to see if they have the attributes for the position.

Wright

You have a new book coming out soon, *How to Be a Power Learner and Make It Pay*. Why did you write the book?

Russell

The motivation came from a student in Michigan who read my Personal Leadership book. His counselor at Central Michigan University called and said, "I want a copy of your book, *The Miracle of Personal Leadership."* I was surprised because I haven't had this book in the bookstores because I've got so much invested in each copy, I lose money when they take their discount. I asked the counselor, "How do you know about this book?" He said, "We had a student we kicked out of Central Michigan University three times for low grades. We let him back in one last time, knowing that he couldn't make it, but to our surprise he made the Dean's honor roll." I asked the student, "What happened to you?" The student pulled out your leadership book and said, "This book changed my life." I asked the counselor, "How did this student get a copy of my book?" And he said, "Well, I don't know." Two weeks later I got an email from the student, he said his aunt who was head of the Arizona Heart Hospital, had sent him a copy. He told me that he had dyslexia, attention deficit syndrome and had never done well in school. He said when was kicked out the last time, his parents wanted him to come home. They were afraid he might do something very serious to himself and that's when he got a copy of my book from his aunt. He said, "This book changed my life." This student went on to graduate from Central Michigan. After that time, he only made one 'B'. Everything else was straight 'A's. He was hired as the Regional Manager for Seven Eleven Corporation in South Bend, Indiana, responsible for eight states. I thought if I never sell another copy of my book, just to help this one student has made all my time and investment in this book worth it. This experience motivated me to start writing, *How To Be a Power Learner and Make It Pay.* There are so many students that drop out of school, who need to be motivated to become life long learners, that could benefit from my Personal Leadership Model to help them be more successful in their educational pursuits. My work with students as a member of the graduate management faculty at the University of Phoenix and teaching at Kansas State University has made me sensitive to the needs of students. I speak at quite a few schools today and have observed the power of student learning, how to lead themselves through the challenges they face in getting a good education to prepare them for life. I decided to write a short easy to read book, *How to Be a Power Learner and Make It Pay,* to encourage students to stay in school and prepare for their careers. Research is showing that if a student will keep learning and prepare properly for a career, they will be able to increase their earnings by one to three million dollars during their life. My purpose is to encourage students not to be school drop-outs and become life-long learners. I also want to motivate parents to understand the Personal Leadership Model and help them encourage their children to stay in school and to succeed in their academic pursuits,

Wright

Why do you say that everyone needs to develop leadership skills?

Russell

The reason is that leadership is so essential today. In a family for example, the parents need to be leaders for their family. About half of all marriages today end in divorce. Leadership skills and especially application of the Personal Leadership Model could have a positive impact in these families. Leadership skills could result in better relationships and stronger families. Everyone, sooner or later, will face obstacles or challenges in their life. Some may have poor health, financial problems, career changes or unemployment. *Success Magazine* said, the average person today will have seven careers in their life. Since I left veterinary practice, I've had eight career changes. Since this is becoming more common today, people need these skills to help them survive the trauma and pain. An American Management Association study revealed that two out of three workers in America believe their supervisors are incompetent. If workers feel this way, how effective can these workers be? Whether it's true or not, if a worker thinks this about their supervisor, it's going to hurt their productivity. I found that one of the biggest problems is people are trying to manage instead of lead. So, leadership skills are essential to be an effective supervisor. Good leadership competencies will assist us to improve our performance, improve productivity, improve relationships and how we influence others. Endira Gandhi said, "Leadership used to mean muscles, but today it means getting along with other people." In today's world everybody would be more effective if they could develop their leadership competencies.

Wright

Is there a difference between organization and personal leadership?

Russell

Absolutely! When we talk about leadership, most people immediately think of being a political, educational, or business leader. You know they are thinking of organizational leadership and that is critical, but in addition personal leadership is very important to lead yourself through the challenges and obstacle of life. I believe if you can't lead yourself, how can you lead anyone else? Personal Leadership is the foundation upon which competent organizational leadership is built.

Wright

Do you have any examples of how people have overcome severe obstacles or challenges by using the leadership principles you teach and write about?

Russell

The story I told earlier, about the student from Central Michigan University, is an inspiration to me. His application of the Personal Leadership Model changed his life. Another great example is my friend Emmett Smith. This is not the football player from the Dallas Cowboys or now the Arizona Cardinals, but the Emmett Smith who was a teacher in the Phoenix area. He ran the 800 meters in the Olympic Trials, but just missed qualifying for the Olympic Games. Somebody said, "You're in the wrong event Emmett, you should be in the marathon." So, he switched events and started training for the marathon. In a short time after he started practicing for the marathon, he became one of the top competitors in the country. It appeared that he would definitely qualify for the next Olympic team. However, as fate would have it, about a year before the Olympic trials, he was diagnosed with a fatal brain tumor.

Only four people had ever been diagnosed with that type of tumor. Two of those four people died on the operating table. The other two were invalids in wheelchairs the rest of their lives. They operated on Emmett, because he didn't have any chance to live if they didn't. He nearly died several times during the surgery, but he survived. Then he nearly died of infection several weeks after the surgery. Fortunately, he did recover, but he was in a wheelchair because he didn't have any balance. Instead of feeling sorry for himself, he said, "One year from the date of this surgery I'm going to run 20 miles." It seemed impossible because he couldn't even walk. He finally was able to get out of the wheelchair and walk with canes. He often fell, but he wouldn't give up. He kept trying until he finally was able to walk so well he threw the canes away. Emmett started jogging along the canal banks. The only problem was the canals often turned, but he couldn't turn, so he often jogged into the canal. Someone suggested that he should focus on a tree or telephone pole when the canal turned and he would be able to turn. This advice worked and he was able to keep from running into the canal. Well, to make a long story short, one-year from the day of the surgery, Emmett Smith achieved his goal and ran 20 miles. Since that time, he has run over 200 thousand miles. His example has been a role model for me. I was feeling a little down after losing that close election to Senator John McCain. I said to myself, "If Emmett could do what seem impossible, what problems do I have? At least I have good health."

Another great example of a young man overcoming serious health problems is the story of Ryan Zinn. When Ryan was 15 years old, he had a stroke. He had to learn to talk again. He missed a lot of school, but when he finally got back in school his heart failed. They had to do a heart transplant, at 15 years of age, to save his life. Ryan was in the hospital 12 days with somebody else's heart. The day he got out of the hospital he went back in school. Just two months after his heart transplant, he was running the 100 meter dash on the track team. He graduated Valedictorian of his high school class and then continued his education at The Ohio State University. He earned his degree in engineering and then went on to receive a master's degree from Ohio State. Ryan competes in the transplant Olympic Games. When these games were held in Columbus, Ohio, he was named the Outstanding Athlete in the games and was written up in Sports Illustrated. Ryan had learned to lead himself through the difficulties of life by being a great Personal Leader. These two friends are a constant inspiration to me. They are living examples that nearly anything is possible if you believe in yourself and are willing to work and apply these leadership skills.

Wright

What did you learn about leadership when you traveled throughout Vietnam on a special assignment from the Vietnamese and American Scouting Association in cooperation with the United States Defense Department during the Vietnam War?

Russell

This was one of the greatest educational experiences of my life. It opened my eyes and made me realize how fortunate we are in America. We take so much for granted in this country. A Scout Leader from North Carolina and myself were selected to travel to Vietnam, during that war to conduct a leadership course. Just before we landed in Saigon, a severe typhoon struck the area this training was to be held, so they had to cancel this leadership course. Since we were on invitational travel orders through the U.S. Department of Defense, the leaders responsible decided we could do the most good by working with youth and civic leaders all over Vietnam. We spent the next five weeks traveling throughout that war torn country. As we worked with these civic and youth leaders, we saw miracles happen. In fact, we'd go into a village or hamlet where children were brainwashed by the Vietcong. These youth might kill or torture brothers and sisters or their parents. We found that villages or hamlets that had any kind of youth programs, such as Boy Scouts, 4H, athletics, etc., they didn't torture or kill their families. All of these programs help develop leadership and character. We take so many of these programs for granted here in America, but in Vietnam these programs were very limited. Wherever they had any type of youth programs, they seemed to be protected from the brain-washing of the Vietcong. This experience taught me the importance of leadership. Another great leadership example was on the outskirts of Saigon. The youth built and operated the first refugee centers. There were many children and families who were homeless and lived in the streets. Members of a Boy Scout Troop saw the need and took the initiative to build and run refugee camps to serve the homeless. Later, adults came in and took over the operation of these refugee camps. I thought, "Wow! These kids are real leaders." In another village near the DMZ, the youth built a barn so they could have youth programs. These young people went out and invited homeless children to come in and participate with them. Some of these children were living in the streets and only ate what they could find in garbage cans. Again, this is an example of unselfish leadership in the purest form.

Wright

Well, I really appreciate the time you've taken with me, Dr. Russell.

Russell

It's a pleasure to talk to you, David. Recalling some of these experience, makes me even more grateful to live in our great country where we have so many opportunities.

Wright

Today we have been talking to Dr. Ray Russell who is the author of the award winning book, *The Miracle of Personal Leadership*. As a leadership coach, his mission, as he stated earlier, is "to raise people and organizations to their highest value," and I think we can see why. Ray, thank you so much for being with us today.

Russell

You bet! Thank you.

About The Author

Dr. Ray Russell, professional speaker, author and executive coach, has served as president, executive director, or board member for two dozen corporate, civic or professional organizations. As a Certified Professional Behavioral/Values/Attributes and TriMetrix™ Analyst, he assists executives improve performance, increase profitability and enhance their quality of life.

Dr. Ray Russell

1550 N. Stapley #21

Mesa, Arizona 85203

Phone: 480.668.7335

Phone: 800.479.3086

Email: ray@executrends.com

www. excutrends.com

Chapter 6

GREG MACIOLEK, MS

THE INTERVIEW

David E. Wright (Wright)

Greg Maciolek, speaker, consultant, author, session leader, has been focusing on the human side of management for almost thirty years. He held senior executive positions for over fourteen years. He focuses on the loss of productivity of workers through their mismanagement by managers and owners. He works with senior executives to ensure organizational alignment and growth and a culture for excellence. He promotes the use of assessments for the hiring and development of all employees in a company. He tells owners that they are "looking for waste in all the wrong places." Greg Maciolek, welcome to *Conversations on Leadership*.

Greg Maciolek (Maciolek)

David, how are you doing? It's good to be with you again.

Wright

Is there a difference between leadership and management?

Maciolek

I believe there is. When I was in the military, I was taught that you lead people and manage things. The leader is the person who sets the vision, the one who is out there making sure they are producing the right product and that they position it correctly and things like that. Thus, the leader looks outward and strategically. On the other hand, managers are those who are in place to ensure that the company functions properly, whether it's accounting or purchasing or manufacturing. That's all part of the management process. Managers look inward and are more tactically or operationally oriented. Leaders do lead people, managers manage processes, but in fact, they manage the people doing the processing. So I think there is a difference.

Wright

Define the role of leader in an organization.

Maciolek

One of my mentors is Gerry Faust, who lives in San Diego. Gerry says, "When you're out there hacking your way through the forest trying to make a path, the leader is the one who finds the tallest tree and looks around and realizes they are going in the wrong direction and yells down "Wrong forest! Wrong forest! We need to go this way.'" When you think about the leader and his role, he is the one who ensures that the company is heading in the right direction, is making the right decisions, and that we're not cutting down the wrong forest, or building the wrong car. Think about Ford Motor Company and the Edsel. Wrong time, wrong car, didn't go anywhere. It's still a joke after almost 50 years. People still label a bad product or idea as being an Edsel. I really think that the role of the leader is that he's not the nuts and bolts of the company, but out there being in charge, or being the rainmaker, or whatever it is that he or she needs to do to ensure that the company continues to do the right things with the right products in the market place.

Wright

Is there a place for managers in organizations? If so, what is their role?

Maciolek

Absolutely. I said at the beginning of this interview that while the leader is out there making sure the company is building the right product or providing the right service, doing the right research, and marketing it effectively, the managers are the ones who make sure that things are done right every day. It is doing the routine things like paying the bills and buying the right materials and having them in place for the workers to build the products to sell. It's human resources helping to hire the right people. It's quality control ensuring quality products leave the plant. That's where the managers exist in an organization. They're the one that have to make sure that stuff gets done. They're not out there deciding what market place we're going to go into. They're not deciding whether we ought to put $10 million into research in this product or service, or things like that. That's not their role. Their role is to ensure that we've got people doing the right jobs at the right times to produce the right product that senior leadership, and I emphasize leadership, has decided that they are going to build. That to me is where the managers play their role. Things don't just happen by themselves. If you don't have those managers in place to make sure that's happening, then I think you run into real problems. Remember where everybody wanted a flat organization? No hierarchy, no bureaucracy. That can work when there are only 5-10 people in a company. However, a company or an organization reaches a point where that won't work. For a business to be successful and grow there has to be some structure to it. You do have to have some hierarchy, a leader and some managers. Because if you don't have structure, if you don't have some of those processes in place, things start falling through the cracks, and that's when you start missing shipping dates, you start missing orders or ship poor quality parts or provide poor customer service. And that's when your customers become unhappy with you. Because you try to keep it too simple, you become disorganized and spend more time fighting fires instead of preventing them

Wright

What qualities or traits should a good leader possess?

Maciolek

Well, there are several. I think, first of all, leaders have got to be visionary. A leader has got to be committed to the vision that he or she wants to attain. Leaders need to look ahead. I don't think visionary people are made. I think there are some unique qualities about visionaries that don't exist in other people. Along with that, I think anybody who has ever run a business, and I know you have, David, you've got to have high personal commitment and high personal integrity to make that happen. Commitment is mandatory if you want to start a company. If you're not committed, your effort will die. It is as simple as that. When you start a company, the company is like an infant. When you have an infant at home, you've got to do everything for that infant, don't you? I mean, the baby can't do anything. Well, that's what happens when you start a company. And that probably means initially working 100 hours or so a week to make something happen. I always like to chuckle when people come to me and say, "Well, hey, I'd like to be a consultant or trainer like you." And I say, "Well, it's a pretty good deal. When you run your own business you can work half days." And they say, "Wow! Man that's what I want to do because now I can play golf in the afternoon." And then I say, "Well, wait a minute, you know what I meant is you have to decide which 12 hours you want to work, and it's not quite so simple." To me, the best leaders I've run into in my consulting work are excellent communicators. They have their vision, and they help to make it a shared vision with the people who work with them. They trust people. They are secure people. And along with being excellent communicators is the fact that they know how to listen. You know the old saying that God gave us one mouth and two ears for a purpose. They listen and because they trust people, they end up engaging the creative juices of the people who work for them. Those are the traits I think are very important. In addition, they need to be a good judge of character. They need to be good at that because if they start infiltrating ill-suited people, especially managers, into the system, their company is going to take a hit. So I would say you need to be a good listener, to empower people, and to have vision, personal commitment, integrity, trust and excellent communications.

Wright

How important is the senior leader to an organization?

Maciolek

How important? They say you can always tell the owner of the company because he or she is the one who picks the trash up off the floor." It's so true because the other people kind of blow by the trash. Thus, the secret for owners is to help create an environment where the workers genuinely feel they are part owners because then they will be picking up the trash too, because it's just as important to them as it is to the owner.

The senior leader is key to the success of an organization. Let's look at a sports example. Let's take a look at the Dallas Cowboys who were pretty dismal last year. They only won a few games for several years after many successful seasons including Super Bowl championships. They had several coaches over the last few years but not one of them could turn the team around. The owner hired a new coach at the end of last season named Bill Parcells. He brought a new vision to the team and they responded. They are 10 and 6 and going to the playoffs. It was interesting listening to an interview with the Dallas Cowboys quarterback, Quincy Carter. He said, "Coach Parcells helped me to believe in myself. He has helped me to understand that I am talented and capable of accomplishing this mission for them, to be the quarterback of the Dallas Cowboys." He says, "He has got me motivated to the point where I come in on my off days to watch films so that I can continue to learn, because I now have so much confidence in myself and that is because of the coach. It's just night and day." What changed? For the most part, Parcells is dealing with the same people that were there last year, right? The coach, the leader, made a difference. Parcells is making a difference in the work ethic and the trust and the confidence of the players that he coaches. This is true for any organization.

So when you think about the senior leader, he's the one, or she's the one who at the very top of that organization starts setting the culture of that organization. When I talk about culture, I'm talking about what is this company like? Do we respect people? Do we appreciate people? Do we honor people? Do we listen to what they have to say? It starts at the top. And the culture affects little things, like "Do we start meetings on time?" You know there is discipline in a company when they say they're going to have a 9:00 meeting, they have a 9:00 meeting and the big guy is there. They don't wait for anybody because this lack of discipline starts permeating through the organization. Well, if it's okay to be ten minutes late for meetings, then it must be okay if we're a little bit late with a shipment. And it must be okay if we go home a little bit early. All that starts at the very, very top. Remember I talked about making sure that the leader hires the right people and brings in the people who are going to help reach this vision, right? Well, this is where you start ensuring that you are putting the right people in place because all that has to permeate down through the management ranks to be sure that they are in fact doing all that stuff and doing it consistently, and not only doing it when the boss is watching. You really have a problem with companies where you start seeing this lack of discipline. Remember when we were kids, our parents would tell us something we shouldn't do, let's say, not smoke, but they would both smoke. Well, we're like little kids. We watch what the leader does, not what he says. I don't care if you are three years old or ten years old or forty years old, if the leader is saying one thing but doing something else, there's a big incongruency. And it starts affecting other areas of the company and its processes. "Well, it must be okay to fudge the travel expense report. It must be okay to do this and it must be okay to do that because this is what I see my leader doing." So the leader becomes ineffective and the company starts to lose.

In my consulting practice, owners of companies will call me up and say, "Greg, can you come fix my people?" I know right away what I want to say to them is "get a mirror because it starts with you." You remember Dr. Deming, right? He was the Total Quality guru who went to Japan and showed them how to do it since we Americans didn't think we needed him. I was privileged. I attended both a four-day and a two-day seminar with him. Here's a guy who's 88 years old at the time, facilitating these seminars. You would think that when he is on a break, he'd lie down in the back of the stage and rest. Not Dr. Deming. He's signing autographs and talking to people. One point that he made during the seminar was that about 85% of the problems of any company rests with management. From my experience, I think that's a low number. I think it's closer to 90%. The duty of the senior leadership, especially the senior leader, is to create an environment where people can excel; where people can be fully engaged doing the things they love to do. And we're doing it all for the common purpose of growing our company so that we are successful and we're providing products or services to the customers out there who need and want what we do. **I see the biggest waste in most companies is the waste of the brainpower and creativity of the people who work there.** Leaders are always looking for waste in all the wrong places and that's because owners and senior leaders look upon employees as assets instead of what they are—**they are the company**. They are the company's competitive advantage. Remember when we were kids we used to use our hands to play "here's the church, here's the steeple, open the door, see all the people?" It doesn't matter whether you're meeting in a storefront or in a huge cathedral, the church is still the people. And this is true with a company. The company is the people, and it really bothers me when I see this slogan on the wall: "People are our most important asset." Because when I see that slogan, I think of machinery and tools. When in reality, they wouldn't have a company without the people. To me, companies do this because they don't have what I consider *enlightened* management. And as a result they cause people to be so frustrated because people want to work; they want to contribute; they want to come in and make a difference. But what happens is they are dumbed down to where they finally get so frustrated that they basically check their brains at the door so to speak. They come in and they go through the motions. Senior leadership sets the pace, the environment, the vision, the plan. He or she needs to ensure that they have *enlightened* managers to carry out the vision and plan. If not, the company will falter, there will be turnover, and productivity and profits won't materialize. The senior leader is the key.

Wright

Can good technical individuals still have successful companies?

Maciolek

Oh, they can but I think they have a little tougher problem. Technical people tend to be more process oriented rather than people oriented. They also tend to look more inward than outward. In other words, they tend to think more tactically or operationally rather than strategically. A lot of technical people aren't always visionary. They often can't see big picture, and that's why they've got to be sure they have some balance in their company. What this type of leader needs to do is to have a second-in-command or a good executive team that possesses the strategic skills he or she may be lacking. They have a big challenge because they also tend to be less assertive and less independent. They love structure and they like precedent too, which affects their decision-making. They sometimes aren't as demanding as may be required to get a company to where it needs to be.

Wright

Why do entrepreneurs have trouble leading companies once they are up and running?

Maciolek

Well, entrepreneurs are akin to revolutionaries. You know you have the people who overthrow a government, and once they overthrow the government, you've got to move them aside because they can't run the government once they overthrow it. The same thing happens with entrepreneurs.

Wright

Right.

Maciolek

They love to get something started and going, but once it gets going, they get bored with it. In fact, if they don't leave, what happens is they start messing with the system all the time and it drives people nuts. If entrepreneurs want to continue running their company, they need to get someone who can help balance them. Someone who helps create some structure, because entrepreneurs don't have a lot of structure. They are out there inventing stuff. They're the idea people, very creative, and they've got these companies going, but then once they get it built they don't know what to do with it. The fun of creating a new business is over and it is time to move on.

Wright

So what do they do to stay involved successfully?

Maciolek

Well, if they want to stay involved with the venture, then that's where the entrepreneur needs to get some balance. They need to hire a good COO who helps run the everyday stuff. The COO is the one who puts stability into the company and make sure things are working and lets the entrepreneur go out and do what he or she does best, and that's probably being a rainmaker, bringing in new business. There's got be someone who can say, "Hey, boss, you're way out to lunch on this thing. We don't have the money to keep doing this and keep doing that." You put some process harness on the owner. If he has that balance, then I think he's okay. Otherwise, he ends up having fights. Usually the entrepreneur says, "Fine, you want to run the company? Here it is and I'm going to go do something else." And the owner sells the company to the COO and his or her team. You read about that all the time. Now what's interesting about that is that when the entrepreneur leaves, if the team that bought the company doesn't have some balance themselves, the company is in trouble. That is because most of the time the structure people buy the company and they lack the vision and creative thinking that made the company a success in the first place. It is like the very soul of the company leaves when the entrepreneur leaves. Unless they bring in somebody who has that kind of leadership ability, the company starts falling down. So it's a very difficult, delicate balance. I find that entrepreneurs get bored after a while and they've got to move on and do something else. In extreme cases, they can be very disruptive to the organization.

Wright

You know we always hear what leaders and managers expect from their people. In your opinion, what should employees expect from their leaders?

Maciolek

I've already talked about the fact that the people are the company and why I hate that slogan about 'people are our most important asset'. What people want is leadership that's going to ensure that they have a company that's going to continue to grow, and that they've got some security. In fact, if they are going to commit themselves to this leader, they need to trust him or her. And they need to know that what they are doing is going to continue on into the future as best as they can tell. Things change obviously, but they want to know that they can trust this leader. When you don't have trust in the leadership of an organization, they are very antsy about what's going on. What workers want is to have an environment where they are fully engaged and you are helping them to grow and stretch. You value their input. They are partners in this game and not just you're the big guy and they are the workers. They want to be recognized for their work. They want to have an opportunity to grow and stretch. I think companies get into big trouble when all the good ideas come only from the top. To my way of thinking, good ideas and creativity have got to come from all levels of the organization.

Anecdotally, I want to compare General Motors and Toyota. I used to work for General Motors in the late '60s. I worked for them for eight years. I worked my way through college as a clerk, and then I became an assembly line foreman. One of the requirements was between January and March of each year, every worker who worked for me, and sometimes I had as many as 55 workers on the line, had to turn in a suggestion. I wrote about 80% of them, because they weren't going to do it themselves. The plant manager had to reach his goal of 100% suggestions from his work force. Now most of these suggestions got tossed because they weren't high caliber. But at Toyota they would get multiple suggestions per assembly line worker and imple-ment most of them. That's how they overtook the Big Three at their own game. Who knows that job the best? The guy on the line of course. When we were working ten hours a day, seventy jobs an hour, it means every 50 seconds we built a car. That assembly line worker was doing that job 600 times a day. However, when we wanted to make a change on the line, we couldn't go to the workers to see how they would improve the job. We had to go to Industrial Engineering. It took General Motors until about the late '70s before they started including hourly workers in the changeover process in plants. Abso-lutely absurd! Workers want to feel that they have something to contribute. When they go home at night, they want to say, "You know what? I made a difference today." If we don't make them feel that way, make them part of the process, we're starting to cause them to check their brains at the door. So that's what workers expect from leaders, and if they are not doing that, they're not setting an envi-ronment for people to excel and they are wasting the creativity of their workforce. A lot of owners don't always think that they need input from the employees because they will tell me, "Well, Greg, we did make two million dollars in profits last year, so I must be doing something right." My answer to them is, "Well, maybe it could have been four or five million!"

Wright

Right.

Maciolek

When workers are engaged and involved, and their needs are be-ing met, the results are higher levels of satisfaction and motivation. You get higher quality and you get much more creativity out of the people.

Wright

Why do you think it's important that leaders hire the right kind of managers to help run the company?

Maciolek

Here's why: if a leader is going to carry out her vision, she has got to have people (managers) who can believe in her vision. And if she is setting this environment as the senior leader, she needs to ensure that the managers below her are doing the same thing. I can't tell you how many times I go into a company, and I see that they have just really hired wrong, or they've promoted wrong. They make people supervisors who have no business being supervisors. That's why I'm such a believer in the assessment process. I think that you can get a pretty good objective viewpoint when you use good valid assessments for ensuring that you've got the people you need. The assessment has to include the cognitive abilities of the person. What is their thinking and reasoning abilities? If you don't select the right managers and engage the managers in the process of carrying out the vision, then the venture won't be as successful as it could have been. That means providing them with the tools they need to carry out their tasks to run their departments. If the owner doesn't trust the managers and allow them to do their job, then they become disenfranchised and dissatisfied. If the managers feel dissatisfied, guess what? Everybody starts being dissatisfied. If I'm working for a first line supervisor who is just completely dissatisfied, and I see him going through the motions, well, what's my feeling about working here? When you take this a little bit further, David, just like people bad-mouth products, they bad-mouth where they work. If they're not happy, they're sitting there at the pizza parlor having a coke and pizza, saying, "I can't wait to get out of XYZ company. Their buddy says, "Why? I saw there was an ad in the paper, and I was going to ask you about it. I was thinking of applying for work there." "You don't want to work there because it's such a bad place." So what happens? You stop getting high quality candidates showing up to apply for work at your company because the word gets out about it not being a satisfying place to work. So companies resort to hiring anybody who fogs the mirror." The reason you're not getting good candidates to show up for the jobs is because you are not creating an environment where people want to work and the people who work there are telling people that. So it does permeate out into the economy and it affects recruiting and retention.

Wright

I'm almost afraid to ask, what happens when leaders don't hire correctly?

Maciolek

USA today ran an article in May, 2000 on Coca Cola, and how the company was providing extra perks like a couple of hours off on Friday and all this other stuff. A lady wrote in about three days later (this was May 9, 2000, I use this in all my training classes) and she says, "When are companies going to get it? People leave bosses not companies." If you're not putting the right managers in place, it affects everything that goes on at a company. While the dissatisfied workers still show up for work everyday, they are not fully engaged. They know exactly what level of work they need to produce to keep the manager from getting on them. So they are working at maybe 65% productivity instead of 90%. What is interesting is that while the worker doesn't get his needs satisfied at work, they get their needs satisfied after work. Many people do volunteer work. They may head up the local PTA. They are the Grand Pooh-Bah of the Lodge. They work in their church. Do you know why? Because people come to them for information and decisions, they respect them. They appreciate them. They are *somebody*. They feel they make a difference. When you don't hire the right managers, people don't feel like anybody cares about them. Let's say you work for a tyrant who only talks to you when you screw up. You go to work and come home and say, "Honey, I had a great day today. My boss didn't talk to me." Isn't that sad? But this is what happens when you don't hire the right kind of managers to help run the company, because they don't understand what's important. They're not sharing this vision of the leader. The opposite is also true. If you don't have a good healthy environment, you could hire some really good people. They are there for about three months and then they say "I don't like the way this ship's being run," and they bail. Who are you left with? You're left with the people who aren't very good to begin with staying on and the good people leaving.

Wright

Do you think that everyone is equipped to be a good leader? If so, why or why not?

Maciolek

David, there's an awful lot of literature out there that says good leaders are made and not born. I don't think everybody is equipped to lead a company. I also think that there are a lot of people who aren't leaders who could be leaders, but no one has ever tapped into their talents. I think that's one of the major challenges of a supervisor. Let's find out what everybody is made of and let's help them to grow and stretch and do whatever it is that they do best. Maybe it's being a leader. Maybe it's being a great manager. Maybe it's being a great press operator. We ought to do what we love to do and use our talents. Take doctors, for example. They can be very good technically but most can't run a business very well. They hire business managers to run their business and they do what they do best—helping their patients to be well and remain in good health. So I think it's more inherent, an inner talent, than it is reading a good book on leadership. But the talent needs to manifest itself.

Wright

Well, what a great conversation, Greg. I really appreciate this time that you've taken with me to discuss what I think is a really important subject and getting more important by the day, in fact. I want to just congratulate you on all your years of success and thank you so much for talking with us today on the subject of leadership.

Maciolek

Well, my pleasure, David, and the best to you also.

Wright

Today we've been talking to Greg Maciolek, who is a speaker, consultant; he's an author, he leads sessions. He has been focusing on the human side of management for almost 30 years, and I think that we've found out today that is very evident. Thank you so much, Greg, for being with us on *Conversations on Leadership.*

Maciolek

Thanks, David, I enjoyed it.

About The Author

Greg Maciolek has been focusing on the human side of management for almost thirty years. He held senior executive positions for over fourteen years.
He focuses on the loss of productivity of workers through their mismanagement by managers and owners. He works with senior executives to ensure organizational alignment and growth and a culture for excellence. He promotes the use of assessments for the hiring and development of all employees in a company.

Greg Maciolek, President
Integrated Management Resources, Inc.
PO Box 31933
Knoxville, Tennessee 37930-1933
Toll-free: 800.262.6403
Phone: 865.539.3700
Fax: 865.531.8897
Email: greg.maciolek@imrtn.com
www.integratedmanagementresources.com

Chapter 7

ROBERT J. DANZIG

THE INTERVIEW

David E. Wright (Wright)

Bob Danzig got his first job as an office boy at a local newspaper 46 years ago. That job turned into a career. Eventually he became publisher of the *Albany Times Union* and *The Knickerbocker News*. He became head of *The Hearst Newspaper* nationwide. Since then, the Hearst group has had a renaissance of talent, technology, and reputation. Annual sales have soared to exceed 2 billion dollars and cash flow has grown 100 fold during Danzig's tenure. An industry leader, Danzig has served the Newspaper Association of America, Newspaper Advertising Bureau, New Directions for News, and American Press Institute. He has earned industry-wide respect for his innovative marketing leadership. A civic leader, Danzig has served on boards of directory of Albany Medical College, Siena College, Russell Sage College, Saint Peter's Hospital, Albany Institute of History and Art, and Caldwell College and on the executive committee of the Saratoga Performing Arts Center. He was awarded one of 12 professional journalism fellowships to Stanford University, the only business executive ever to be accepted into this program. He now serves on the board. Danzig graduated with high honors from Siena College in Albany and later received its award for outstanding career achievement. In May, 1997, Siena College conferred on him an honorary Ph.D. He is author of two books, *The Leader Within You* and *Vitamins for the Spirit*. Mr. Danzig, welcome to *Conversations on Leadership*.

Robert J. Danzig (Danzig)

Thank you very much, David. I am delighted to be with you. Let me just amend your comment, I've now written five books.

Wright

As author of *The Leader Within You*, what are the nine powers of leaders that you describe in that book?

Danzig

I really describe powers that are evident in so many leaders who crossed my path during the course of my career. While there are many powers that people may ascribe to leaders, those that struck me most were these: their commitment to quality, their spirit of innovation, their capacity for inspiration, their passion, their perseverance, their character, their charisma, their energy, and their enthusiasm. Those are the powers I think you will always find some combination of in leaders.

Wright

Do you favor any one of those powers?

Danzig

I happen to favor one because of my growing up in the foster care system where you really put all of your energy into survival as you move from home to home. I never had a family, therefore, my energy was put into that survival. That survival can often mature into perseverance. My favorite power is perseverance because I feel that strength is characterized in me and it came from the adversity of growing up in the foster care system.

Wright

How frustrating is it growing up in the foster system? It's really changed in the past couple of decades?

Danzig

Well, it's a challenge. You can imagine as you or anyone listening to this program or reading this book as you reflect what it means to be part of a family. When you're not part of a family you are detached. You just have a little black, plastic garbage bag—now they give them duffel bags—but you're shuffled from place to place and you're without anchor. Therefore, when good people cross your path and invite you to gain anchor from them, it can change your life.

Wright

So, what is the goal of the kids in the foster care system? Adoption?

Danzig

Most of them have adoption, but adoption is very difficult in the United States because of each state's legislative requirements. You and others may know many who have adopted children from China and Chile and Korea and Romania and you wonder why because there are 588,000 kids in the American foster care system. Adoption takes up to four years and is fraught with all kinds of legal infirmities and hurdles here in this country, so these kids end up being very dispirited about the prospect of adoption. It does happen, but not often. We have five children and our fourth child is adopted, but I know many, many kids who end up only drifting through the foster care system, as I did.

Wright

My minister has adopted two children and is trying to adopt one more even as we speak. He says the money is what will really pull a lot of people down. He said it costs about $30,000 upwards.

Danzig

That's to adopt a child from another country. I'm not sure that is the same hurdle here. It's a problem of the legal system where a person may adopt a child and then three or four years later a parent that abandoned that child will show up and demand parental rights. It's fraught with difficulties and it does frustrate these kids. Eighty-five percent of the kids in foster care never go to college. Only 15 percent ever go for any higher education. It's amazing that they have persevered through this because they have never had consistent support you think about the things that represent family values and living a life without any of those. That doesn't mean that foster care parents can't be empathetic and interested and concerned, but it's not the same as having a natural parent.

Wright

With these nine basic principles that you have adopted here, commitment, innovation, etc.—one stands out in my mind. That's the issue of character. It seems like over the last few years character has really come into question—especially in the corporate world. Could you speak on that?

Danzig

Of course I can. One of the great things about our system is that not all, but many of these situations that end up being egregious lapses of character end up on what I call the "store window." They end up being revealed by the media and suddenly course corrections begin to occur. That's been the story of our society for a few hundred years now. Something may grow to be excessive, like a lack of character or excessive greed, but then there seems to be a bursting of that bubble and then you have course corrections coming back on. In my experience, running a very large multi-billion dollar company for 20 years, is that most leaders are effectively embracing good character. They are not like these exceptions. I think these are the exceptions and I am not among those who condemn the private enterprise system or the others—like the Catholic Church. Look at the Catholic Church and the challenges they've had with so many priests being accused of being pedophiles. That doesn't mean that there aren't a lot of good people embracing that church also. I think that we're in the process right now of that course correction, and I hope that the ultimate effect is to cause people to have more confidence in our system.

Wright

What do you think lifted you from office boy to nationwide leader of Hearst Newspapers?

Danzig

The goodness of people who crossed my path and took an interest in me. One was a social worker when I was 11 years old who was moving me to yet another foster home. At the end of our little discussion, she took my hand and said, "I want you to never forget that you are worthwhile." No one had ever said that to me before. No one had ever said that I was of any consequence whatsoever. Her name was Mae Morris and every time I met with her, she ended our discussion the same way—always telling me to never forget that "you are worthwhile." It became what I call a tattoo on my spirit. It lifted my whole sense of personal possibility.

My first boss, when I became the office boy at the newspaper, was a very tough little lady named Margaret Mahoney. I had worked for her about four months and one Saturday morning we were covering the complaint phones together in the circulation department. She called me in her office and she sat me down. I was terrified of her. She said, "You know, I've been the office manager here for 15 years and I've been observing you. I believe you are full of promise." That was magical that someone in authority, particularly a woman because foster care kids are raised in a matriarchal society, said to me that I was full of promise lifted my whole sense of self. I never stopped hearing her words. I went to college nights for 6 years. Seventeen years after walking in the door as the office boy, I was head of this very large company. We had 972 employees and a big, big operation. I never stopped hearing her words. Seven years later, I was in New York running the whole of Hearst Newspaper nationwide and I became President of Hearst Newspapers. I never stopped hearing her words, "You are full of promise." When we are open to the good people who cross our path, those can become the beacon lights to guide our own development and growth. That's what happened to me. There are many others like them, but those stood out. So, I think the key, David, is to be open to the leaders across your path who want to give you the gifts of their wisdom and insight.

Wright

What are the softer values that you've come to sense in effective leaders today?

Danzig

What I notice in really effective leaders is that they have a mindset of possibility. It starts with their mindset. They are personally motivated. They don't require others to turn on their own engine of motivation. They have an attitude to do more than is required. They are in the habit of going the extra mile. The single attitude that you find most often in effective leaders is the softer value of doing more than is required. The final is that they are conscious of the value of building self-esteem among those that they are privileged to guide. I find mindset, motivation, attitude, and self-esteem awareness to be critical to effective leaders.

Wright

I knew a man in Texas many years ago when I was beginning my career of running businesses. I had about 125 people working for me. I met him at a conference and I asked him basically what you just said. I was kind of angry one day and I said, "So who motivates the motivator?" He looked at me and he said, "You do, or you'll never be a leader."

Danzig

That's what it boils down to.

Wright

You write about celebrating success. Could you share an example or two of how you did that with a national company with colleagues so geographically apart?

Danzig

Well, again, David, under the general guise of your mindset, my mindset was that we may be a multi-billion dollar company, but what makes us that is the values of all talents who chose to give us their best. I would have a system. Any day I was in New York city, where my offices are, and not traveling, my long-term assistant of about 23 years would send an e-mail out or a fax out to our operators around the country that said, "Bob's here today." They knew that by four o'clock that day they were to have back to me the name, the address, the spouse's name, and one sentence describing what some individual in the organization had done that was worthy of a compliment. Marge Murphy, my assistant, would organize all of these names and addresses, I would take them home on the train and write a note to every one of those people on my personal stationary thanking them for what they had done for our company. I would mention the specific thing they were doing that was furnished to me by that newspaper whether it was Houston Texas or San Francisco or Seattle or my hometown of Albany, wherever they were around the country. If they were doing something extraordinary I would put an "F" next to one name or a "T" next to another and Marge Murphy knew that flowers were to be sent to the spouse of that person with a note that just said, "Congratulations on the news." For example, if you were one of our colleagues, it might say, "for your David." Who would ever reason to celebrate your success at home where you were loved? The "T" was for her to send a bracelet from Tiffany's. If it was a male spouse, she would send a key ring. Those people get the same message, "Congratulations on the good news for your David." I got in the habit of doing this and I wrote to hundreds and hundreds and hundreds of people. In every one of our operations, every one of the senior managers was conscious of and looking for ways to celebrate their colleague. Even though I might be in New York, 3,000 miles away, those people knew that I knew they mattered. Every person that got a note or a Tiffany gift or flowers would tell all of their colleagues. That built an aura of celebrating success.

Wright

Boy, talk about a personal touch. What a great story! Is it your conviction that leaders are born or are they created? How do they come about?

Danzig

I believe they are nurtured by being open to the people that cross their path. I believe that all of those powers that I just mentioned that you find in leaders are in every person. They are available to be discovered and burnished and polished and mastered, but some people choose not to do that. That's okay. Not everyone can be a leader. They're making a choice to settle for less than their ultimate fulfillment, in my view. I'm a great believer that leaders are formed by being open to the circumstances around them and they seek ways to make a contribution. It's never about personal success. It's always about ways to make a greater contribution. That's what you'll find in leaders.

Wright

I was told by someone many years ago that if I thought I was a leader and I looked around and no one was following me, I was only out for a walk. You know, he made the point that this thing about being a leader was something that you earned from your followers. Would you agree with that?

Danzig

I do agree with that. You'll find, David, that leaders are always effective communicators. They work at connecting with people. The words of an organization as well as the behaviors of the leaders are what build the marrow that causes people to be comfortable in following you. They have to know from your conduct that you know they are worth while, that they're sharing to give their talent with you. They're choosing that sharing.

Wright

Can you describe some leaders who have left a lasting impact on you?

Danzig

Yes. Certainly, one was the publisher of our newspaper in Albany, his name was Gene Rob and he was a giant of a man, a great leader. He was a lawyer and very articulate. He also had a genuine concern for other people. He would take the time to be attentive to the people in the organization who needed that attention. I took note of that. I sat next to him for several years. He died prematurely which is why I became publisher so very young. The fact was he was sponsoring me for the fellowship at Stanford University. I was astonished when I got it, but I did. It was not his brilliance. It was not his clear communication ability. It was the fact that he had a general mindset to care about the people. I was one of those people. I can remember when my wife had the first of our five children. My bride had come down with toxemia and he studied toxemia. He got information about toxemia and told me the kinds of things we might consider doing to ease her through this difficult time. He also told me to go spend my time with my wife, rather than worry about my business obligations. I never forgot that. I never forgot that as a great leader he never failed to take the time to care about the people around him. That's not paternalism. That, to me, is a caring nature. I've also been exposed to so many others who were so effective. The common threads are all of those qualities I mentioned in my book.

Wright

Are managers the same things as leaders?

Danzig

I think there is an enormous difference between the two, David. So often, organizations settle to be only or mainly managed. When you're mainly managed—here is the distinction between the managed place and the led place. Management is about today. Leadership is about tomorrow. Management is about process. How do we churn out books or whatever it may be? Leadership is about purpose, noble purpose and understanding that purpose. Management is about feeding the body of a place. You have to be able to do that. We have to be able to pay the 6,000 employee colleagues of the Hearst newspapers. You've got to do that. Leadership is about feeding the spirit of a place. Whenever you find a place that excels rather than simply functions, it is excelling because it's got an eye on tomorrow, it understands its noble purpose and it nurtures the spirit of the organization. Managed places tend to coast over time and nothing ever coasts uphill.

Wright

How does the leader maintain the spirit of a business?

Danzig

By being attentive to the people who create the business. By understanding the noble purpose. By sharing that with conviction.

Wright

You're saying noble purpose.

Danzig

Noble purpose. Here you are in the publishing business. You could be just churning out books. You could be a producer of books. You could have a production operation. But, when you have an idea for a book, just like the idea for this *Conversations on Leadership*, there's a noble purpose. Of course, you hope it's going to be a business success. Of course, you hope it will be helpful to the contributors, but it is a noble purpose that the ideas contained within that book are going to have the prospect of enriching, guiding, lubricating someone's life and career. That's a noble purpose. That is true in every single business. You have to ferret out your noble purpose. We're going to produce and distribute 11 million Hearst newspapers around the country this week. We're not in the business of producing and distributing Hearst newspapers, we're in the business of communicating ideas, of representing progress in the community we serve, of producing an instrument to care and nurture that community. That's the difference—you're not about just producing things but about producing things with a noble purpose.

Wright

I've just extended my personal definition of leadership. I ask so many people that question but you never get anyone saying anything about a noble purpose. The definition before that I carried around with me was that the difference between management and leadership is vision. But, vision without noble purpose is—for example, the point you made about the publishing business. If I really wanted to make money I'd probably be publishing pornography.

Danzig

You make a good point. As I mentioned, I've authored five books. I just finished a two book package, one is called *Every Child Deserves a Chance* and the other is called *There is Only One You*. When I have an idea for a book, I write out the noble purpose. I write that out. I let it be the guiding statement as I go about the book.

Wright

By the way, how do our readers and listeners find these books? Do you have a Web site?

Danzig

I have a Web site. It's www.bobdanzig.com. The books are available on Amazon.com, at Barnes & Noble or any bookstore. If they don't have the books in stock they can order them. And we have, as I say, five books. The last two books each include a song CD that I commissioned by some gifted artists in Nashville. The only way to get the CD is with the book.

Wright

That's interesting.

Danzig

One of the songs is called You Are Worthwhile, You Are Full of Promise and the other is called There is Only One You.

Wright

Who are the people who left the most indelible impact on your career?

Danzig

Well, first, my bride. We'll be married 46 years this Summer. I met her as a youngster. She was in college, I was not. I was just a classified ad salesman. But, she has been the source of inspiration that caused me to choose to lead a life rather than simply manage a life. I would have never gone to college without her encouragement. I probably wouldn't have gone out to Stanford for that fellowship because our daughter was very ill at the time. I was very happy running that newspaper in Albany, New York, our hometown, but she said to me, "You must go to New York and take over this company because you will give it your best and you will change their destiny." So, she has been a tremendous influence on my life, a constant influence. She was also the one who encouraged me to step down early to become a professional speaker and write books. It's all because of her. The other people are that publisher in Albany, that first social worker who encouraged me by saying I was worthwhile, and that first boss who said to me, at 16, "You are full of promise." Imagine here I am all these years later running a multi-billion dollar company for two decades and I still hear their words in my mind. The other was the CEO of the Hearst Corporation, Frank Benneck Jr. He was an outstanding leader, a great visionary, a great communicator, and he had wonderful empathy. I can remember, David, when my daughter Marsha who is now a young adult had bone cancer in her leg. We had to agree to amputate her leg. I was up in Boston at the Children's Hospital. I was overwhelmed by the circumstances and I called him to let him know that I would have to stay there for a little while to get everything straightened out. His comment to me was, "Only you can be the father of your daughter. We can run this company. You stay there until you're satisfied that your parental responsibilities are filled." That's a great leader.

Wright

Let me ask you, is leadership very important to an organization or can a well-managed place do just as well?

Danzig

Well, as I alluded to earlier, well-managed places tend to mainly function, David. They never excel. They simply function. They function adequately. We've acquired many, many business that functioned and they functioned adequately, but they never reached the higher level that they were capable of. That only happens when the talent of a place is ignited to give you its best. That's caused by the spirit of the organization and spirit is ignited by effective leadership. It's really a very simple equation. Managed places function adequately. Well-led places excel consistently.

Wright

Boy, what a difference that is. What impedes some people from embracing the opportunity to lead their lives, their businesses, their futures?

Danzig

I think that people often choose what I call the lower road. They choose to avoid the aura of responsibility, the cloak of taking on responsibility. They don't teach themselves to be comfortable with that. Therefore, they settle for mediocrity. Mediocrity to me is toxic. Once you start settling for mediocrity, you end up with a mediocre life, a mediocre business, a mediocre career. There's no reason to do that. You can have excitement, a sense of enterprise, a sense of fulfillment, a sense of achievement by choosing to embrace a higher road to whatever extent you can. It's no different than a person's spiritual life. You can choose to live a life that is barren of the influence of a higher power. You'll live life, but it'll be a barren life. You can live a life that recognizes the influence of a higher power and you'll have values, you'll have judgment, you'll have morality, you'll have decisiveness, and you'll have a sense of growth. The same thing happens to people's lives in business. They just choose the lower road. We're not meant to do that. We're meant to choose the higher road. I'm a guy with no childhood, no background, no money, nothing going for him who ended up being the head of one of the largest newspaper companies in America and I hope, a reasonably effective leader and the author of five books. It has to be because someone encouraged me to walk the higher road.

Wright

What a great conversation we have had. I've learned so much today. Bob, I really appreciate this conversation with you. You don't know how much I appreciate the time you've taken today.

Danzig

It's been my great pleasure, David, and I hope that we get the chance to get to know each other better.

Wright

Today we have been talking to Bob Danzig who started as an office boy and become head of one of the largest newspaper companies in the world. We have found out some of the reasons why today. What a leader you'd be. I wish I worked for you.

Danzig

Thank you very much, David.

About The Author

Robert J. Danzig is former, 20 year— nationwide CEO of multi-billion revenue, 6000 employee Hearst Newspapers. Cash flow grew 100 fold—not percent, but fold—during his tenure. Author of *The Leader Within You, Angel Threads, Vitamins for the Spirit, Every Child Deserves A Champion and There Is Only One You*. He began his career as a 17 year old office boy, became Publisher by age 33, then to Corporation as entire Newspaper Company CEO. He attended college nights and is now a member of the teaching faculty of New School University as well as Journalism Fellow of Stanford University. His speaking topics include: Common Powers of Transformational Leaders, Threads of Life, Softer Value of Success and Tools of the Confident Leader. Mr. Danzig is Dean of The Hearst Management Institute—the Corporation's internal executive development program and executive coach for senior managers who wish to be more effective Leaders.

Robert J. Danzig

Phone: 212.649.2178

Email: bdanzig@hearst.com

Chapter 8

MARIANNE SMITH EDGE, MS, RD, LD, FADA

THE INTERVIEW

David E. Wright (Wright)

Today we are talking to Marianne Smith Edge. She is a sought after and compelling motivational speaker, consultant and businessperson. Marianne's achievements as a business executive, author, public speaker and leader in her community, statewide and national organizations allow her to captivate and relate to any type of audience. She brings more than 20 years of practical business experience to each of her presentations that include leadership, management, and healthcare. She is the owner of MSE & Associates, LLC, a nutrition management consulting company that provides services to healthcare facilities and corporations through the country. Through her seminars, Marianne Smith Edge provides her audiences with interpersonal understanding of leadership and management challenges, ideas to meet those challenges, and the motivation to put the ideas to work. Marianne, welcome to *Conversations on Leadership*!

Marianne Smith Edge (Smith Edge)

Thank you.

Wright

How do you recognize and mentor potential leaders?

Smith Edge

Potential leaders have an enthusiasm for what they are doing and are always willing to give their best effort. You can recognize their leadership qualities by the true passion they exhibit. You often see these qualities in people involved in professional or volunteer organizations. Aspiring leaders are prepared to be a servant leader, one who recognizes that a shepherd would not have a job without the flock.

Wright

Do they just pop out or do you have a talent to see them?

Smith Edge

If you are looking for leadership in an individual then you are more in tune to the qualities that make them a potential leader. It is very important that when you identify these qualities in an individual that you encourage them to develop their skills and commit to leadership functions in their respective profession or organization (be aware that some are quieter than others, you might call them internal leaders), but they still possess leadership abilities. If possible become a mentor. We all have busy schedules, but mentoring can be done through voice mail, e-mail or just a note of encouragement. I believe most people possess strengths that can move them to leadership positions, but need the encouragement to pursue them.

Wright

So leaders are born? In other words, does leadership come naturally?

Smith Edge

Some people do possess more of the strengths and skills that will move them into leadership positions, but I concur that the term "born leader" is a myth. Possessing these skills does not project one into an "instant leader." It is important to learn to "lead" yourself before trying to "lead" others. Those individuals who are willing to step up and accept the responsibility for leadership have acquired knowledge from many people and circumstances throughout their lives. But, a true leader commits to a path of life long learning.

Wright

How do you perceive issues of gender bias? What are some of the strategies you suggest to overcome or maybe take advantage of it?

Smith Edge

The whole gender bias issue is very interesting and most frequently we think the bias is against females in a male oriented industry. However, in the healthcare environment it is often the opposite due to being a predominately female oriented industry. I think that in either of these situations where one gender is predominant it may be difficult to break into a leadership role. But, it is important to understand that it's a cultural issue not a personal bias and we should not enter the environment with a chip on our shoulder. You have to recognize when you are a female entering into a male dominated organization that you may have to work harder, initially, just for acceptability. That doesn't mean that you have to become "like a male" or give up your personal qualities, but you do need to understand the "rules" within the environment. Finding commonalties among genders tends to overcome perceived barriers. In fact, in today's younger generation there is less perception of individuals being denied leadership positions related to gender bias as they have witnessed more cultural/gender diversity in the workplace.

Wright

Why do you think that certain healthcare professionals have moved more quickly than others have into management positions?

Smith Edge

Historically, some healthcare professionals, such as nurses, have had more opportunities for leadership positions due to the perception of the system that they possess a more broad base understanding of the industry. Likewise, these positions have been equally open to utilizing their skills outside of traditionally trained models. However, all allied health professionals possess the qualities of critical thinking and evaluation skills that are vital characteristics for a leader. It will require allied health professionals to seek opportunities and take initiative to apply and accept responsibilities outside their traditional training if they desire management/leadership positions.

Wright

What are critical thinking skills?

Smith Edge

The ability to assess and evaluate a situation and implement treatment or solutions. Healthcare professionals receive extensive training in reacting to situations quickly and efficiently. They must be able to assess situations for underlying causes and react appropriately to resolve issues through application of appropriate treatments.

Wright

Are there any unique traits or characteristics needed for leadership in the healthcare industry?

Smith Edge

One of the key traits is a real passion to serve people. Most individuals who have entered the healthcare field have an underlying desire to serve and understand the need for providing quality care. This desire, in addition to some of the critical thinking skills, provides an excellent foundation for understanding people and their needs. To be an effective leader you have to be aware of the needs of people. Healthcare professionals have seen people at their worst and in many cases helped them to become their "best."

Wright

Can women leaders "have it all?"

Smith Edge

I think this is a discussion that will continue into infinity. In Carol Gallagher's book, *Going to the Top*, she interviewed over 250 women CEO's about "can women have it all." Some said "yes" and others said "no, you have to make choices." I think it is very difficult as more is expected of women. A woman who decides on a career path typically has to make personal choices about family issues, whereas with men this has never been as much a part of their career decisions. But roles are definitely changing as men and women become more adaptable to the needs of the family situation. Many times the woman has to make the final choice. If you really commit to a career then a great deal of juggling of personal and work schedules is required. It is a matter of choice and you have to be willing to work hard and make sacrifices at times.

Wright

Is there still an acceptance issue with spouses or significant others or peer groups?

Smith Edge

I think in some situations there is. I am extremely fortunate to have a very supportive husband who has never been intimidated by my career. But, if you look at the role models around him you can understand his philosophy. His mother and sister are both professionals and I think this has made my career choices more acceptable to him. In some cases perceptions of the traditional role of a woman in our society still exist. I know women that are not always complimentary of other women that have decided to combine career and children, thinking that the "working mother" isn't always doing what they should for their children. They are basing their opinion on traditional models to which they have been exposed. Times have changed and will continue to change as there are more "working moms." These women are developing the skill of multi-tasking—a quality definitely needed in leaders.

Wright

I noticed that you own your business and have hired many people down through the years. I always like to discuss, especially with females, what is going to happen when you start making more money than your husband. I have even asked the husbands. They all laugh and say I wish she would double my income. But, in reality, almost every time that has happened, at least in my experience, it has caused great turmoil in the family.

Smith Edge

Personally, incomes haven't been an issue in our 21 years of marriage. My husband always says, "I'm looking forward to the day when your career will allow me to retire." I truly believe he is very serious about that. He is very successful in his own right and a very balanced individual. However, I do believe the subject of income earnings and personal perceived value does need to be discussed among couples. I think the issue of women earning more than men within a relationship continues to decline as "double income" families are more common.

Wright

What is your philosophy on leadership and the development of a leader?

Smith Edge

One of the quotes from Bennis' early books on leadership: "Managers do things right, but leaders do the right thing" describes my philosophy. I believe that a true leader is someone who makes the decision for the good of the organization, not for the good of themselves and realizes that the "right thing" may not always be the most popular decision.

Wright

How did you evolve into a leadership position?

Smith Edge

As a child I was involved in the community, church and service organizations. My parents were very committed to the philosophy of volunteerism and this probably set the course for me as a professional. Working in professional organizations in my community and state level led me to positions nationally. Also, having mentors who recognized my leadership qualities and encouraged me to pursue the next level provided opportunities for me. This goes back to identifying potential leaders and mentoring them. I think the key is if the door is partially open, peek in and be willing to jump in and say "I'll do it." After that, stay committed to the task.

Wright

We talked a little bit about whether or not leaders were born or whether they came by it naturally. The perceived fact that there are born leaders has proven to be a fallacy in theory. What are your thoughts on this?

Smith Edge

As was mentioned earlier, I do concur with the fallacy. There are not necessarily born leaders. The "born to lead" fallacy was developed in the era when you only had the opportunity to lead if you were born into the right family or class. I think everyone possesses the ability to lead, but one chooses whether or not to hone these skills. Some individuals probably could lead major groups or organizations, but really choose not to. Or, they do it in a much smaller, quieter way. So, do I think everyone is qualified to be President of the United States? I think there are definitely more individuals who possess the leadership skills to lead a nation, but resist due to the environment one must lead!

Wright

You spoke a few minutes ago about mentors. With our *Conversations on Leadership* book we are trying to use the examples of our guests to help our readers to be better and live better. What do you think are some of the characteristics that make up a great mentor?

Smith Edge

I think the individual that has the characteristics of a good mentor is one who really sees an individual as a potential leader either in a volunteer or professional setting. They are willing to take the time to help a person and give them opportunities to hone their skills. At the same time, a mentor must be able to offer words of encouragement and help mentees recognize that everyone makes mistakes. A good mentor is someone who is willing to give his or her personal time, expertise, and encouragement as well as constructive criticism.

Wright

You know I hear a lot of people talk about how great it is to have a mentor. I have found that sometimes I have received the most joy from looking into a life that is less than it should be as far as self-esteem is concerned, or not realizing their own potential and seeing something in them that they do not see in themselves, and for that reason helping them to develop. So in that respect, the mentor is the one that receives the joy.

Smith Edge

I totally agree. Sometimes you may not realize how much of a mentor you have been to an individual. Last week at a meeting I met a professional that was an intern with me four years ago. She said, "You know, I wouldn't have chosen the path I did if I hadn't worked with you and your consulting firm before I graduated from college." This truly is a major reward. It is important to understand that mentoring is one of the qualities of being a personal leader, leaving a legacy, a strong foundation around you.

Wright

You said a lot of things about leadership, but is everybody quali-fied to be a leader?

Smith Edge

I believe all people have some leadership skills. But, as we said be-fore, some have chosen to develop these skills and others choose to be followers. I have always said that in leadership positions there are two kinds of people: floaters and swimmers. A floater is one that is willing to go along with the current, be on top, be seen, but not really diving in, or making any waves. They consider leadership as a "name" entitlement not a service. They tend to be in a leadership position for themselves, whereas, swimmers are more the servant leader. Willing to work hard to make things happen, go against the current and do whatever it takes to make the organization a success. A successful leader has the vision and passion to "stay the course" even when sharks get in the way!

Wright

Well, what an interesting conversation on leadership, especially from a female's point of view. That's always refreshing. Today we have been talking to Marianne Smith Edge who is a popular and compelling motivational speaker, consultant, and businessperson. Marianne, thank you so much for being with us today on *Conversations on Leadership*.

Smith Edge

Thank you. It's been a pleasure talking with you.

About The Author

Marianne Smith Edge, MS, RD, LD, FADA, is President of MSE & Associates, LLC. Her company has evolved from long term care consulting to encompass diverse ventures—professional speaking, private practice with a specialty in food allergies and mental health to partnership in Dialogs for Leadership. She is President of the American Dietetic Associaiton (2003/04), serves on the Kentucky Licensure Board for Dietitians & Nutritionists and is a member of the University of Kentucky Board of Trustees.

Marianne Smith Edge, MS, RD, LD, FADA

MSE & Associates, LLC

516 Ford Avenue

Owensboro, Kentucky 42301

Phone: 800.572.7647

Fax: 270.688.0949

E-mail: msedge@smithedge.com

www.smithedge.com

Chapter 9

PHILLIP FULMER

THE INTERVIEW

David E. Wright (Wright)

Today we're talking with Phillip Fulmer, whose first decade as head coach of the Tennessee Volunteers could be classified as the best ten-year period in the school's glorious gridiron history. He led the football team to a national championship in 1998 and also was named National Coach of the Year that same year. In 2000, Coach Fulmer received the second annual State Farm Eddie Robinson Coach of Distinction Award. This award is given to a coach for being a role model and mentor to students and players, for being an active member of the community and for being an accomplished coach.

The University of Tennessee has posted ninety-five victories under Coach Fulmer against just twenty losses since he was named head coach in 1992. His winning percentage of 82.6 percent also places him ninth all-time in Division 1A, alongside such notables as Newt Rockney, Frank Leahy, Barry Switzer and Tom Osborne. In fact, he's the only coach in the top fifteen on the all-time list who is still active. His efforts have been especially fruitful of late. Tennessee has led the SEC over the last five years with a total of fifty-two victories.

Coach Fulmer is the author of two books, *Legacy of Winning*, written with Gerald Sentel, and *A Perfect Season*, written with Jeff Haygood. Coach Fulmer brings a relaxed but motivational style to corporations who want to inform and inspire their employees and keep customers with game plan success. He does a lot of speaking throughout the United States. Coach Fulmer, welcome to *Conversations on Leadership*.

Phillip Fulmer (Fulmer)
Thank you very much.

Wright
Coach, many corporations today find one of the biggest challenges to be creating an environment of success in the workplace. When you speak to the business sector, how do you advise companies to do that?

Fulmer
I think one of the most important factors is taking the role of a leader, setting the standards high and guiding all of the employees down a path of distinction. In other words, everybody in the organization knows the goals that are set and the attitude that it's going to take to get there. In our case, we tried to establish an "all for one and one for all" type of attitude and work with our long-term goals in mind on a daily basis. I think it's extremely important to have that as an atmosphere within the family, if you will.

Wright
Do you have great communication with all your assistant coaches? What are your methods of communicating with them?

Fulmer
I think we have great communication. That's a very important part of what we all do to be successful. You've got to believe that the team is the most important factor. In our situation, we're dealing with different maturity levels with youngsters and often strengths and weaknesses and environmental issues. Formulating that into the team concept takes great communication. My leadership role is to give them the foundations and the paths to follow along the way. My assistant coaches and all of the support groups should simply be an extension of me and us. It's best when you have that consistency and that communication level going. Most of the time, you are successful.

Wright

The Sporting News, one of sport's most prestigious magazines, has written of you: "He's a player's coach and a solid motivator. Fulmer is the nation's best coach." What do you think it means to be a player's coach?

Fulmer

You know, I had some concern about that initially, because I thought that perhaps that made me sound like I was soft. But after maturing some myself in the position, I think that it means that there is mutual respect and that it runs both ways. I think the players know the consistency that I expect from them, the effort that I expect and the off-the-field expectations as far as academics and social behavior go. We touch on the spiritual attitude of the young man, because I still think he's in a developmental time. In return, they know that they can expect the same determination, the same efforts, the same examples set by me and my staff. When you're working with that kind of relationship, I think it could be called "being a player's coach." We're not dictators, we're mentors. We're men who are trying to help adolescents grow into men. We take that approach, and it's been successful for us.

Wright

Coach Fulmer, your record indicates some little known facts—at least little known to me. For example, you had a total of sixty-four academic All-SEC honorees in four years, including nineteen in 1998. With all of this talk about college football being about business only, do you believe there's a correlation between an excellent student and a good athlete?

Fulmer

I don't think there's any question that if your team has good players, they are also better students, dedicated and hard working. That doesn't necessarily mean that they're all going to be rocket scientists or anything like that, but they're determined to have success. If you have more players like this than your opponent, you are more than likely going to win. I do think there's a correlation between success and academic achievement. You're here to be a student athlete. The truth of it is that we are, in some ways, a springboard to the National Football League for some athletes that are very skilled. You certainly can't say that they're not successful when they make $5 million-a-year salaries. For the most part, there is a very limited number of guys who are going to be able to do that. The rest are out there to prepare themselves to be employers, employees, citizens, husbands and fathers. We take that role very seriously and expect the players that we have to also take it very seriously.

Wright

To follow up on that question, are academically excellent student athletes easier to coach than students who are not? Will these traits not follow them in the business life after football?

Fulmer

No question. We're all very interdependent on each other. The guy who's the self starter—the one who's going to get up and have breakfast, get to that 7:50 am class, makes sure that he gets to that study hall in the evening, uses the tutor and does all of those things—is going to be the guy who will be out there hustling and will be the early bird getting the worm. I don't think there is any question that the background taught by their parents and reinforced by us is going to pay great dividends in the future.

 Wright

You've stated that the development of good citizenship attitudes is compatible and consistent with team goals. What opportunities do you give your players for community service and involvement?

Fulmer

We have gone as far as to hire a full-time staff member, Jim Harrison, who's responsible for public relations and community service for our football team. He does a tremendous job of helping our young people. I think it's so important in their short term growth that they feel like a part of the community and that the community feels good about them. In the long term, the communication skills and the appreciation for what they have in college are important; often they are dealing with people less fortunate than they are. We require each player on our football team to do at least one thing per semester in the community. Obviously, a lot of our players are more high-profile players and do a tremendous amount more than that. But overall, we're very active in giving back to the people. We have tremendous support at UT and we feel like we're a part of the community. We feel an obligation. Speaking somewhat selfishly, I think that when they're out there reading to a fourth grade class, visiting a sick child in the hospital, going to an old folks home, speaking to a D.A.R.E. group or whatever, it makes them more accountable and more responsible for their actions. It has paid great dividends for us as well.

Wright

I can remember growing up in the Knoxville city school system. Back when I was in the fifth or sixth grade, I can remember people like Doug Atkins and Jimmy Hahn—I think it was the 1951 national championship team—coming over to our grammar school and teaching us to square dance. I will never forget that.

Fulmer

I don't know if any of our guys will be teaching square dancing, but I'm sure they could teach the dances that are out there now.

Wright

You just don't think of Doug Atkins, that giant of a man, helping a fourth or fifth grader learn how to dance.

Fulmer

It does make a significant impression. I remember the same thing when I was a youngster. Ronnie Warwick, who was a great linebacker for the Minnesota Vikings, came to our school and spoke and actually spent some time. At that particular time, he was the only guy I had ever asked for an autograph. I still have it. It had an impact on me. He told his story and I figured out that if he could do what he had done, considering all the struggles he had gone through, it was something that I could do too. I hope our kids are motivating young people to go out there and try to be successful.

Wright

As an offensive guard at the University of Tennessee from 1969 through 1971, your team's record was thirty wins and only five losses. Since there are so many players in the sport and so few coaches, it must take a different set of skills to coach. What do you think it takes to be an excellent coach?

Fulmer

I think you have to be multifaceted in today's world—a leader of men, but also a communicator, not only with your athletes, but with your staff, the administration and faculty. Then you have responsibilities with the boosters and the fundraisers and all those kinds of things, so you have to be a great communicator. I think it helps to be positive. I'm one of those guys who says the glass is half full most of the time. We're going to find a way to get it done. I think that's extremely important. You have to be able to manage your time and get your priorities in order to allow you to be successful and make the best use of your time. I learned the hard way that you still must remember your family. My first couple of years, I was so determined to make it work that I think I drifted apart from my children and my wife. I made a really hard effort to get back and catch up on those years that I missed and spend quality time with my family. I think that as a tactician and a strategy guy, you've got to be able to plan for the future, figure out the problems before they get too big and change with the times. We've been able to do that with our studies and research. Recruiting is, obviously, a very valuable tool, and that goes back to the communication skills and hard work. Once you get a good player to the campus, it's really a matter of developing those skills because everybody recruits good players. It's the kids who are most disciplined and the most physically developed who then mature. Usually the teams with the most juniors and seniors are going to be the teams that are the most successful. That requires that you develop your skills and spend quality time, having that relationship so that they're going to respond to what you ask of them.

Wright

On more than one occasion, I noticed your daughter by your side on national television as you ran to the middle of the field after a game. How hard has it been to raise three daughters and a son, given all of the time demands that you've had since becoming head coach?

Fulmer

I'm very blessed to have the children. My son is thirty-two, and I missed a lot of time with him. But my girls have been with me at my side. It was my wife's idea to put them at the sideline with us. I was concerned about what they might hear or that they might get hurt, but it's been one of the greatest things for them to share in those exciting moments—and there have been a lot of them—and even in the few disappointments that we've had. For them to be there and be a part of what's going on has given them an appreciation for what Daddy does. I think, again, it goes back to the core values of our program and that's one of the ways that we demonstrate that family is important—that we're all there for each other and that we'll be there whether it's the best of times or the toughest of times.

Wright

As you mentioned, recruiting is extremely important. Besides obvious athletic ability, what characteristics do you and your staff look for when recruiting?

Fulmer

You begin with character, which I think is extremely important. We tell our guys that we want character in our program, not characters. Guys are going to go to class and they're going to be in the weight room when they're supposed to be. We're not going to have to worry about what they're doing in the evenings. Of course, college is a growing time and there are a lot of problems out there if guys want to get into them, so they have to make great decisions that way. We talk about them being line touchers—who is going to touch the line when the coach is not looking. We talk about those kinds of things as a staff before we offer the scholarships. It's really easy to see the guy in the film who's going to be the next great player, athletically, because of his size or skill. We call them twenty-footers because you only have to watch about twenty feet of tape before you realize this guy is really special. But you've got to find out a lot more than that. Academics, character, the environment, what their goals are, where they come from, what I can expect as far as stability, ability in the young man and how he will take discipline when it comes down to it—we discuss all of those things thoroughly.

Wright

When I interviewed Vince Lombardi Jr., he said that his father's greatest strength as a coach and a man was his faith in God. The elder Lombardi was, of course, a legendary coach and that surprised me a little. Through the years, has faith played an important role in your decision making?

Fulmer

I don't think there's any question that that's been probably the key issue in my success. I was raised by a wonderful mom and dad in the church. Men in the community who gave me exposure to the Fellow ship of Christian Athletes (FCA) also tremendously supported me. FCA gave me the opportunity to go to Black Mountain, North Carolina, Lake Geneva, Wisconsin, and Snow Mountain, Colorado to FCA camps. My faith grew there and I was joined with other people of different denominations from around the country who were also athletes. It allowed us to bond and have a support group with each other. My wife is tremendously faithful as a Christian lady. My children have grown up, thank God, to be the same way with the same values. We have made mistakes along the way. We're certainly not perfect by any stretch of the imagination, but the faith that we hold together is the bond in our family. I believe it is also the bond in our program. We look for that in young men—not a particular denomination or anything like that.

Wright

I suppose the true test of the influence that a coach has over the athletes that play for him is whether or not they stay in touch with him through the years and still call him by that revered name "Coach." Do you keep in touch with your former players, and do they still seek your advice and council?

Fulmer

We stay in touch quite well, I think. Obviously, you have some that are more special than others just because of the relationship that you build and all of the things that you go through while they're there in college. Particularly as an assistant coach, I still have a great bond with a whole bunch of guys that I got to know as a position coach. Then as a head football coach, I have really learned to make sure I take time to touch base with all of our captains and all of the leaders on our football team along the way. Peyton will pick up the phone and give me a call. Or it might be Peerless Price. Last night at an alumni event, I saw Bubba Miller, one of my great linemen from a few years ago. You might not have seen them for five years or even have talked to them for a year, but when you see them it's like it was just yesterday.

Wright

Coach, I have a last question for you. If you could give America's leaders advice on how to be successful leaders, what would you say to them?

Fulmer

We talked about core values earlier. Establish what the core values of your organization are going to be and don't veer far from those. Communication is also tremendously important because many times we all want the same end, but we might take different paths in getting there. Sometimes, it might be one of those paths that takes you a lot farther than it should. I think discipline is extremely important. We often hear, "Coach, you do a great job of recruiting." And we do. But I also think that we do a great job of coaching and developing those skills in those young men and having discipline in our program. We are never too far away from our core values.

Wright

Coach, I sincerely appreciate the time that you spent with me today. It's been fascinating, and I've really learned a lot.

Fulmer

Thank you for your time. I appreciate it.

Wright

Today, we have been talking to Phillip Fulmer, whose first decade as head coach of the Tennessee Volunteers has been absolutely fantastic. Many think he's the greatest working coach in football today and many others I know believe that he's one of the finest men that they've ever seen. I think we've learned that today. Coach, thank you so much.

Fulmer

My pleasure.

Phillip Fulmer is completing his ninth season as head coach of the Tennessee Vols and has continued to add to the list of accomplishments that have placed him in the top ranks of his profession. First and most important to fans of the Vols has been his status as the nation's No. 1 coach in terms of winning percentage. Tennessee's 8-3 regular-season mark in 2000 maintained Fulmer's won-lost ratio margin as No. 1 compared with his peers. But, it was off the field last fall that Fulmer received one of the most prestigious and personally satisfying honors that can come to a man in the field of athletics. A blue-ribbon panel of judges named Fulmer the second annual winner of the State Farm Eddie Robinson Coach of Distinction Award. Named after famed Grambling coach Eddie Robinson, the award honors an active college football coach who demonstrates the qualities that exemplify Coach Robinson's legacy–a role model and mentor to students and players, an active member of the community and an accomplished coach.

Phillip Fulmer

www.PhillipFulmer.com

Chapter 10

DR. ISABEL PERRY

THE INTERVIEW

David E. Wright (Wright)

Dr. Perry brings motivation to an all-new level. Her audiences are energized by her "can-do" attitude and transfer their newly gained skills into success. Dr. Perry, welcome to *Conversations on Leadership*.

Dr. Isabel Perry (Perry)

Thank you, David. It is my pleasure.

Wright

Tell me, what is the impact of terrorism and workplace violence on employees?

Perry

In recent years, the workplace has undergone an emotional upheaval. In the 20th century, "workplace safety" often referred to protecting employees from hazards created by machines and the materials individuals used to perform their jobs. However, in the 21st century, the scope of "workplace safety" has expanded dramatically. Leaders now have the added responsibilities of keeping the workplace safe from terrorism and workplace violence. These two elements create more anxiety and stress for employees nationwide, as well as worldwide.

Unknown risks and the element of surprise contributes to a considerable amount of emotional uneasiness and greater distractions for everyone at all levels of the organization. Leaders are expected to plan ahead for new situations that have not yet been identified. Employees are concerned about their personal well-being and that of their family, who, most likely, are at a different location the majority of the day.

There is another major element that contributes to additional stress, distractions and uneasiness in the workplace......we have become "news-junkies." There is a tremendous desire to be on the leading edge of news, especially bad news. Because of the uncertainty in the world, individuals want to protect loved ones as soon as possible and "herd into the family unit."

As a result, morale, productivity, and focus drops in direct proportion to the amount of negativism and potential injury that may impact the employee and/or their family. This creates all new issues for leaders in the workplace.

Wright

So, how can a leader keep morale high and people focused?

Perry

Let's look at morale, first. Never before has it become more critical for leaders to be visible and manage by walking around. This is leadership in action: spending at least 15 to 30 minutes a day communicating directly with employees. People want to know there is a captain of the ship and someone is in charge and addressing potentially risky situations.

Leaders must learn to share more information with others and increase the level of communications between and among the layers of the organization. People like to feel included in the inner circle of information; a sense of "being included" always ranks in surveys as one of the top three criteria of what makes employees happy.

Find some good news to share with others. Certainly, there is *something* positive in the company that can be shared. Employees and associates will be delighted to share positive news with each other. That optimism spreads and multiplies, because enthusiasm is contagious. Gradually, morale will increase and the emotional hemorrhage of "negative events" will lessen. Being optimistic is not a short-term fix, but rather an ongoing business style to increase morale and productivity among others.

Another way individuals can build a positive atmosphere is to speak with energy and enthusiasm. Demonstrate cheerfulness and friendliness. Compliment others on something they are doing right, even if it's just a routine task. If nothing more, just smile.

Make sure employees know the importance of their job. Describe how their individual role and contribution to the organization fills the pipeline for the company's success and affects decision-making. Convince them that they *do* make a difference, and that their focus and execution of their responsibilities are critical in building a strong foundation for the organization's stability and future growth.

Ask employees for ideas and then *listen* to them. Effective leaders must possess good speaking skills, and also good listening skills. Let them talk; being heard is good therapy for building self-esteem and self-confidence in the organization. It is healthy for individuals to share their thoughts and knowledge with leaders. It is also beneficial for leaders to hear the grass root issues, concerns and potential solutions to obstacles in the organization. In addition, there may be "gems" of break-through thinking in those conversations; it is critical to listen.

Another way to boost morale is to increase the peer recognition program. This could be an announcement or publication in the company or department newspaper of an employee's accomplishment, milestone or award, either within the company or in volunteer activities outside the organization. Numerous studies show that praise and recognition go much further than monetary rewards, which are usually forgotten in less than a week. These are only a few of the hundreds of methods a leader could use to increase employee morale.

Now, let's discuss the second part of your question, "How do we keep employees focused with so many distractions?" Employees want to have peace of mind that emergency programs are in place and all measures will be taken if an untimely situation should arise. This would include programs and plans for natural, as well as man-made disasters, terrorist threats, and workplace violence.

When leaders share the organization's strategic plans and goals on how emergency situations will be handled, employees feel comforted that someone at the top is listening and there is a plan for defensive actions to reduce their personal risk. Employees want to know that someone is addressing the issues and cares about their well-being. If the negative situation hits close to home, or is a part of the company's world-wide operations, it is critical to keep employees informed of countermeasures the local facility would take, should the incident occur at their location.

In times of crisis there can never be enough *accurate* communication. Being honest and being sincere can never be underestimated. Members of the organization will follow strong leaders who exhibit, confident, thoughtful, decisive and resilient behavior. In addition, employees are more likely to stay focused on their tasks.

Another way to keep people focused is to praise their deeds and accomplishments, rather than the person individually. This is a greater motivator because by complimenting the person, individuals will constantly wait to have verbal praise given to them. Whereas, if completed tasks are complimented, completion of the task is the motivator. Individuals will learn to be focused and will be driven to work on accomplishments or meeting deadlines, because *that* is the motivating force, not verbal praise.

Building meaningful goals with time driven milestones is another way to encourage individuals to remain focused. When projects are more structured and built with a plan, individuals will reference their plan more frequently. This method keeps the focus on the plan to reach the goal, rather than lesser distractions and environmental "noise."

Wright

So, how can leaders solve problems and make decisions quicker in a crisis situation?

Perry

Problem solving and clear, decisive decision-making are skills that separate strong leaders from the others. Successful leaders do what unsuccessful leaders are afraid to address. They achieve the almost impossible by not being afraid of challenges, risk or the unknown. They realize that they cannot wait for 100% no-risk solutions. They cannot afford over analysis of certain information, while other issues sit on the back burner.

Leaders can improve their decision-making skills and derive at better conclusions by making priority setting a priority. Setting aside time for priority setting is a discipline that will pay off well in emergency situations and improve clarity of thinking. Therefore, when a crisis situation does arise, more accurate and decisive decision making skills are demonstrated. It's been said, "Plan your work and then work your plan" for maximum performance.

In order to move or motivate an organization in the right direction during an on-going crisis situation, a vision and goal must be established. This information needs to be communicated so people know there is strong leadership at the helm. Individuals will follow decisive leadership and flounder under weak leadership. The leaders must control and dominate the negative situations or crisis or it will control and dominate them. Decisions need to be addressed quickly and head-on. In crisis situations to NOT make a decision, is to make a decision. There may be higher risks making decisions quickly with less information in a crisis, but at times, the situation may call for bold action.

Another technique used to make decisions quicker is to NOT allow the staff members to use their leaders as a crutch for *unnecessary* guidance; this weak behavior may become a habit and will reduce the amount of productive time from others. Although a team atmosphere is applauded, overuse of this environment can create lazy thinkers and can become a crutch for some employees who lack self-confidence. Employees should be encouraged to bring solutions to their superiors. A recommended technique would have employees develop a list of options to a problem situation, with a top priority. Then, the options can be presented to the leadership and critiqued for their merit. A recommendation and final course of action should be the conclusion of the discussion. This activity helps to develop self-starters and fill the pipeline with future leaders that possess self-confidence and crisp decision-making skills. This is part of succession planning to better serve the organization in crisis or non-crisis situations.

Another method to build quicker decision making skills is to learn to eliminate distractions, which will enable better focus. Leaders must delegate routine tasks in order to provide a quality, uninterrupted and focused atmosphere for strategic and systems decisions, which are more complex. However, delegation of routine tasks is just half of the puzzle. Employees need a clear understanding of the vision that will enable them to determine what information needs to flow up or throughout the organization and provide data for more strategic decisions throughout the organization.

Another important skill to develop for crisp and better decision making before crises or emergencies is to not attack the messenger of bad news. If you attack the messenger of bad news, they will not deliver negative information; and sometimes, negative data provides the complete picture of the total situation. If critical information, albeit negative, arrives late, decisions and course of action may need to be revised at the eleventh hour.

Better decision-making is made when strong leaders surround themselves with individuals who are willing to go the extra mile and do more than just what is required of them. It is advisable to select people who have demonstrated that they are able to cut to the chase and remove the "noise of irrelevant data" surrounding the issue. These are individuals who have the ability to motivate others to follow them in accomplishing goals. Leaders should observe future leadership candidates in action and conduct behavioral audits to identify tomorrow's superstars.

A final method leaders utilize to make decisions quicker is to constantly ask themselves if what they are doing "in the present" is the best use of time for the long-term goal. Spending too much time on putting out fires, and not enough time building strategies and systems, is a recipe for constantly being "in crisis" and handling emergencies poorly. Manage time wisely and focus on plans and systems or the organization will remain in a reactionary mode.

Wright

So how does a leader build followship in times of crisis?

Perry

People love to be respected. Use the *Platinum Rule*, which is a higher level than the Golden Rule..... "treat others as YOU wish to be treated." Rather, the *Platinum Rule* teaches us to "treat others as THEY want to be treated." By motivating people and showing respect for their criteria, we build followship. Others flock when there is a comfort zone. Take the time to be in their work area and be seen. By communicating a vision, providing others an idea of direction for the group and describing what that situation would look like, others will follow and continue to promote the idea, plan or program.

President Kennedy did this when he said we were going to the moon by the end of the decade. He communicated a vision and where he wanted to go; people followed. The leader must define the vision, but it's the subordinates who define and deploy the objectives and move the organization to the desired outcome.

Wright

What do you think are the qualities crucial for leaders today in an uncertain environment?

Perry

The basic qualities of leadership, such as honesty and intelligence...to name a few, are the foundation for success in normal times. A few other traits are crucial for leadership success in crisis situations. The first is courage; the courage to make a decision in a quick manner, perhaps without all the answers. The courage to empower, trust, and depend on people in the field to make the right decision. The courage to think outside of the box in creative ways to solve new and unusual problems. The courage to address problems and attempt goals that really stretch the envelope and have never been addressed previously. The courage to make unpopular decisions. The courage to deliver sad news. Courage is *critical*.

Leaders must demonstrate enthusiasm and energy, which are additional qualities needed in a crisis situation. Consider the symbolism of the design of the Pearl Harbor Memorial in Hawaii. The length of the monument is seen as a smooth, continuous concave curve with both ends being higher. The architect wanted to express the sentiment at the beginning of World War II; our momentum and enthusiasm were high. During the course of the war the momentum and morale lowered. Then, with our successes in various battles, we regained our enthusiasm and energy and won the war. If at the lowest point of morale in the war, our generals had become discouraged and acted defeated, the architect may have symbolized the monument differently. So, enthusiasm and energy are crucial in tough times and also, very contagious.

Credibility is another quality that is necessary in times of crisis. Credibility is similar to a bank account; it must be there before you need it. Leaders will depend on their "credibility bank account" to influence others quickly in times of crisis. Everyone can increase their credibility by possessing high values, standards, ethics, honesty and trustworthiness. By working at building credibility constantly and embracing new skills and competencies, self-confident, self-esteem and credibility become the result. Only with a high credibility level is an individual able to influence and lead others.

Wright

What new programs and policies should be in place?

Perry

Whether it is terrorism or natural disasters, every organization should have an *"Emergency and Disaster Management Plan."* This is part and parcel of the Homeland Security efforts ongoing in our country. In addition, a *"Workplace Violence Program"* should be implemented to address internal emergency issues with personnel.

Wright

What are the key elements of an emergency and disaster program?

Perry

An emergency and disaster program is a written plan designed, deployed and periodically tested that outlines specific actions to be taken to reduce risks and minimize losses under crisis. The plan is based on critical and thorough review of potential emergencies or disasters pertaining to the facility. This includes natural, as well as man-made disasters.

There are four stages in building the plan. First, a planning team, composed of a cross section of individuals within the organization, must be established. These individuals bring various skill sets with them to help establish the skeleton framework of the program. This knowledge may include emergency response communications skills, facilities equipment and availability, etc. A team should never be composed of "like" people because they will offer similar solutions and answers.

The second step is to analyze the types of hazards having the greatest potential to affect the organization. This is called a vulnerability analysis. Build scenarios around each category of incidences. And, based upon the risk of each scenario, follow the probable course it will follow and probable damage that may occur. Then the list of scenarios must be prioritized. Questions that could be answered to set priorities include: What types of incidents have the have the greatest likelihood of occurrence, such as fire or explosions? What outside assistance can be utilized? What situations are least likely to happen, but would have more catastrophic results, such as chemical or biological attack?

The crucial step is to develop the plan in written form. This includes, but is not limited to, identifying the emergency response procedures for each situations....fire, explosion, bomb threats, etc., establishing in the incident command post, addressing facilities needs such as emergency power supply system, building communication matrixes within the organization, as well as to employees homes, and ways to co-ordinate with outside organizations. The communication and distribution of this plan to all "area leaders" is imperative. It is advisable to put the Emergency Plan on the company's intranet for easy access in crisis situations.

The last step is to implement and test the plan. Conduct training, ensure good communications within the organization, as well as to local authorities. Evaluate the effectiveness of evacuation routes, assembly points and accountability systems for the whereabouts of all employees. Only by testing and evaluating an emergency system can is be deemed effective.

Wright

What are the key elements of a Workplace Violence Program?

Perry

There are four major components to an effective workplace violence program:

1. Management commitment and employee involvement
2. Worksite Analysis
3. Hazard Prevention and Control
4. Training

Let's examine each of these briefly. First, both management and employees need to work together, perhaps in a team or committee approach. Management must support and commit to implementing and providing the resources for the program, such as medical and psychological counseling. In addition, responsibilities and obligations must be assigned to members at all levels of the organization. Employees must report violent incidents promptly and accurately. Together both groups must develop a written program.

The second major component of a workplace violence program is Worksite Analysis. An evaluation of the workplace is necessary to find existing or potential hazards for workplace violence. Examples of the methods used to gain this information are reviewing injury and illness reports, monitoring behavioral trends, conducting screening surveys and analyzing workplace security.

The third element of the Workplace Violence Program is Hazard Prevention and Control. Methods must be designed and implemented to control the hazards identified in the previous step. This could be through engineering controls (i.e. closed circuit video for high-risk areas, bright lighting indoors and outdoors), and administrative controls (i.e. report all incidents, create liaison with local authorities, and adopt a zero tolerance policy). In addition, the post-incident response and evaluation are essential to an effective violence prevention program.

The fourth major element of a Workplace Violence Program is education. The training must include all employees with a discussion of their responsibilities, the factors that cause or contribute to assaults, a typical action plan to various situations, and more.

Wright

How does a leader handle media interviews during a crisis?

Perry

First and foremost, a leader should perform the initial job of "communicating" the situation. This demonstrates credibility and authority over the situation. When dealing with the media, never lie, deceive, or distort. All these situations can cause turmoil in the future. If there is any information that is incorrect, set the record straight as soon as possible. In dealing with the media, seek to understand the intent of the question before seeking to respond and be understood. By using this technique, the response will hit a bull's eye, not just the target. Before answering tough or threatening questions, take time and be conscious of body and facial language.... the slightest grimace, can be distorted as meaning something unintended. Keep emotions neutral and speak with surety.

To appear less aloof, make eye contact with the person or the camera and speak directly to the issue as if talking with a friend and explaining the situation with them. When giving an interview or when answering questions, do not criticize anyone. Criticism is the fast route to losing professional credibility. If crucial information cannot be divulged, it is best to NOT answer with "No comment." Rather, state why that information cannot be shared at this time and why. State the information can be shared when the situation warrants its release. It is also advisable to add that further details will be shared when possible. In extremely volatile situations with legal implications, prepare a written statement, read it, and end by saying, "That concludes my remarks." Advise the media that they will be notified when more information becomes available. Exit, before the situation becomes a media frenzy.

Wright

You know, a lot of the people in the country—and I may be one of those people—wonder just how much time and effort our leaders, in corporations especially, give to these things that we've talked about here today. We're talking about spending a lot of time in training and giving your people a lot of knowledge, for example, dealing with violence in the workplace, making it a safe space. As you travel around, are the people who are actually running our corporations really interested in doing these things?

Perry

Absolutely. Progressive companies are dealing with "safety beyond OSHA" in the workplace because they know the foundation for their growth lies in the productivity of their people. We all use the same equipment when we're manufacturing a widget, but it's our people that make the difference. If our people are distracted by their concern for a safe workplace, they are not focused on their jobs. As a result, they are less motivated and less productive.

Yes, of course it takes more time to add new programs and discussions of these programs to the workday. However, consider this; we all have a pie chart with 24 hours in it. Today there is a little wedge of responsibility in our 24 hour time clock called "safety, emergency and disaster planning." Organizations must deal with how they are going to address these crises. Leaders will be at the helm of some of these activities and depend on their staff to handle some of these new programs. Certainly, there may be people in the organization whose contribution has risen due to the results of September 11th and due to all the workplace terrorism we're experiencing. Unfortunately, I don't believe the violent situations will lessen. Leaders must step up to the plate and build systems to reduce the potential risks that lie ahead.

Some organizations will rush to get "back to basics" six months after an act of workplace violence or terrorism hits the headlines, without addressing the root cause and preventative measures for a recurrence. These organizations are constantly in a mode of "putting out fires" and working in a reactionary mode in ALL areas of their organization, including responding to competition. Organizations that do not respond to risk have the greatest amount to lose in uncertain times. Poor planning results in crisis management. Fortunately, for the future economy and strength of our country, these groups are becoming fewer and fewer.

Wright

Violence aside, there's something you said that I thought was very important. I have dealt with some of these problems in my business life. You said that if I take an employee, any given employee, and put myself in the middle of that employee and the task that I want to be done, in other words if I make them or let them come to me to make the decision every time, I actually build weakness into them?

Perry

Exactly, because if employees know they can rely on others to solve their problems, they will continuously avoid making decisions. This is similar to a child who never grows up, matures and builds any independence. By continuously solving routine problems for others, leaders weaken their own staff. Individuals avoid taking responsibility and become increasingly dependent on others. The ability to empower and delegate is lost. Part of business maturity is teaching others to make decisions based on relevant data provided and to take ownership for those decisions.

For extremely difficult decisions that have impact throughout the organization, I coach individuals to approach their boss by:

1. Stating the problem
2. Stating the possible solutions and the consequences of each
3. Prescribe the best solution and give justification on why that is the best conclusion.

If the leader allows their staff to put the responsibility for decision making on their back, that is a lot of weight to carry at the end of each day and the leader will burnout. There will never be enough hours in the day for the leader.

By using this technique, the employee builds greater confidence and the organization builds a stronger pipeline of leaders who make solid decisions, based on fact, not emotion.

Wright

So a lot of trainers just stop at saying we need to delegate. I always felt very uncomfortable with that statement alone. Just, "David, you must delegate." I know how to delegate, but a lot of times, because I thought it was the personality of the person that needed some affirmation or something, I can see where I was their crutch.

Perry

Exactly, leaders need to bank their personal energy reserves and stamina for more strategic decisions. And, the leaders need to communicate their expectations of this style of management and the various levels of decision making empowered to their staff. Some individuals are timid about making decisions; perhaps earlier in their careers they were micro-managed by someone who made ALL decisions. I've always taken this position.... "I'd rather have them ask for forgiveness for their occasional mistakes, than permission." Organizations don't want to build stagnant departments that are immobilized by their inability to make effective decisions.

Companies should want to encourage others to take action, make decisions, and move forward. If employees are always asking permission, the leaders will never get their work done because others are in their office requesting a "permission slip."

Wright

When you talk about leadership, are you including supervising, managing, and that sort of thing? Do you differentiate between management and leadership?

Perry

Leadership can be found in all levels of an organization. Let me share an example from September 11. A number of men were stuck in an elevator at the World Trade Center. Society would rank the suited executives as leaders in that small space. However, the window washer took the leadership role because he was familiar with the environment and the building structure. The elevator was stuck between floors and he knew that on the other side of the elevator doors there was a solid wall. After the elevator doors were pried open, the window washer used his window squeegee to scrape against the wall and dig away at the surface to bore a hole to the other side. He directed the others to take turns. Suddenly a team was formed and everyone was taking direction from their new leader, the widow washer. He was the person most familiar with the environment and the corporate leaders yielded to his knowledge. The window washer was successful.

Often, leadership roles bounce around in an organization to the person with the knowledge of the topic. Individuals need to set their egos aside, and use the most valuable information, regardless of its source.

Wright

I can find all kinds of instances where that would happen in the corporate world, but we just get so used to calling one person a leader and everyone else a manager or supervisor. It seems a little unfair to the employees.

Perry

I think leadership can be found at all levels of the organization, it is not limited to those at the top of the organizational charts.

Wright

Well, what a great conversation. I've certainly learned a lot today, and I want to tell you how much I appreciate you taking all this time to talk to me about this really, really important subject.

Perry

Well, thank you for giving me the opportunity, David. I appreciate it.

Wright

Today we have been talking to Dr. Isabel Perry who is a highly motivated professional with the unique combination of experiences as a corporate executive, an entrepreneur, an author and a speaker. Thank you so much for being with us today on *Conversations on Leadership*.

About The Author

Dr. Isabel Perry is keynote speaker, consultant and writer on the topic of "safety." She has 25 years of broad based experience in the field, including that as a safety, health, environmental and security executive in a Fortune 50 Company. Dr Perry is the founder of TheSafeytDoctor.Com, Inc., a full-service safety organization with international clients.

Dr. Isabel Perry
"The Safety Doctor"
Orlando, Florida
Phone: 407.291.1209
Fax: 407.291.7499
Email: Isabel@TheSafetyDoctor.com
www.TheSafetyDoctor.Com

Chapter 11

GEORGE HEDLEY

THE INTERVIEW

David E. Wright (Wright)

Today we're talking to George Hedley, often referred to as the "Profit-Builder." George is a recognized expert on growing a successful business. He founded and built his $75 million construction and development company and received the nationally recognized *'Entrepreneur of the Year'* award. Today, along with managing his company, he owns HARDHAT Presentations. As a Certified Speaking Professional he helps business owners and managers always make a profit, develop leaders, create loyal customers, build wealth, and get their businesses to work. He is the author of *On-Purpose...On-Target!* and *Everything Contractors Know About Making Profit.* George Hedley, welcome to *Conversations on Leadership.*

George Hedley (Hedley)

Thank you for this opportunity.

Wright

How does the current business climate affect business leaders?

Hedley

Over the last several years, the entire business economy, whether it's service or products, retail or wholesale, every industry—has been growing at a slow and steady pace. This while the overall market capacity of suppliers, manufacturers, installers, and service providers has increased at a much faster pace. The output capacity of all companies is now greater than ever, but overall market growth hasn't kept up. In other words, companies need to do more to stay even. Competition is growing, market share decreases, and the pressure to sell at lower prices increases.

But how can companies do what they need to do to thrive? It is very difficult for leaders of successful companies to make radical changes in how they have been doing business over the last ten to twenty years. Companies become entrenched in their business models and infrastructures as their owners and leaders become older and set in their ways. Business leaders know they need to adjust for less profitable sales, lower prices, and less customer loyalty as profit margins shrink and competition becomes more intense. Today the only way to be successful, thrive, and do better than your competition in the years to come is to do business radically differently than you have in the past. To keep doing business the same way you've done it in the past is another way to cause slow death.

Wright

Is increased competition here to stay?

Hedley

Absolutely! Business is changing quickly. Big business continues to wipe out the little guys, the dot-comers come and go, manufacturing moves to China, services get subcontracted to Western Europe or India, public companies driven by the need to grow revenues continue to diversify and buy up smaller local companies, and the internet continues to level the playing field for bargain hunters and cost cutters. These global factors cause business output capacity to continually increase rapidly while the total market demand grows at a slow and steady pace. This equals major price erosion for every business, even the small local companies, contractors, suppliers, service providers, retail stores, and manufacturers.

Wright

George, what is the number one factor to owning and building a successful business today?

Hedley

The number one problem with business is that business leaders, managers and company owners continue to be stuck in the past. They fail to realize squeezing out the last drop of productivity, cutting their overhead to the bare bones, trying to cut costs, working harder, and continuing to try to do business the same way with the same old customers, won't cut it today. I believe when companies don't get the results they want, it's not the competition, the economy, or their people, it's the leader!

The leader is responsible for everything—sales, profits, growth, quality, customer service, how organized the company is, people, management, etc. The buck stops with the leader. People tend to blame poor or stagnant results on circumstances out of their control. Most want to sit and wait for the economy to turn around, or some other miraculous event while they don't do anything different or decisive. Leaders have to make it happen. For example, look at what happened to Sears dominating their market. They can blame their slow death on Wal-Mart, K-Mart, the economy, or whomever they want to. But in reality, the leaders of Sears made decisions to stay the course, do business the same way they always had, and not change their business model. The leaders hoped their new and different competition would go away. The leaders didn't do what they needed to do. Therefore, they got eaten alive and now they continue to scramble to keep up with their competition. It won't happen. It's too late.

Wright

What do you think leaders must do to get continuing results?

Hedley

Leaders must realize results are the main indicator of their performance as leaders. It's not the economy, their people, or the market conditions. Real leaders make quick and decisive decisions to change how they do business to get the results they want. Most leaders and managers don't walk into their office on Monday morning and say, "I've made a big decision. I've made a decision to change me and how I lead." Poor leaders walk into their office and say, "Why aren't you making it happen? You've got to work harder or smarter. You've got to do this now or that next." Leaders must have the courage to change themselves first. They try new ideas, change their behavior, change their markets, do something different, innovate, try a different method, and go against the grain.

Over ninety percent of employees rate their company leadership below excellent, according to a *Fortune* magazine survey. The top companies have leaders who continually look for areas of improvement, new markets, and new ways to be different than their competition. Their people want to follow them and they make results happen. People follow people who have integrity and lead by example—people they trust. It's kind of hard to trust somebody who's not doing what he says others should do. People want to work for people who appreciate them for who they are and what they contribute. That's the starting point to getting results—trust and appreciation.

Wright

What is your definition of "Profit-Driven Leadership"?

Hedley

Several years ago I authored the term "Profit-Driven Leadership." I speak to a lot of conventions, small to medium size businesses, construction owners, manufacturing companies, etc. The common question and challenge they face is how to always make a profit. Making above average profits and getting bottom-line results start with the profit-driven leader having a really dynamic and focused vision people can get excited about. People want to be a part of something exciting and want to follow leaders on a mission.

Profit-driven leaders stand up and say, "Here's where we're going and here's how we are going to make it happen." People want something they can really, really get excited about, instead of the standard: "Work hard and we'll see how it comes out; and if we do well, maybe we'll give you bonus or a raise." People get tired of doing the same thing over and over without any excitement, vision, or passionate leadership—like digging a long ditch for a long time. And, when they're done, they just get another ditch to dig. And then when they finish with that ditch, their boss finds some more ditches to dig. This doesn't make people excited about coming to work and making a difference in the bottom-line.

Profit-driven leaders start with an exciting focused vision and then connect it to the specific results they want. Some companies have a vision to be the best company, the best contractor, the best service provider, or provide the best quality. While that's an O.K. vision, it's not exciting. An exciting vision might be to be the recognized leader in customer service in their target market area. After defining your exciting vision, specific results must be targeted to quantify exactly what is expected. For example, if your vision is to be the best service provider, determine what specific measurable results really enhance your bottom-line. Some target ideas include: a referral from every customer, only five percent callbacks, no installation errors, or 95% on-time completion. What specific targets and numbers can you shoot for to realize your vision & get the results you want? Without specific clear targets and defined results, none of your people really know what "to do your best" and "to be your best" really means.

Go ask your people who work for you, "What's the vision of our company? What are we trying to accomplish? What are the three top priorities we are trying to make happen?" You'll get 57 different answers if you have 57 people working for you. You must get everyone on the same page from top to bottom to get the results you want. It's like in baseball; every player knows the deal. The object is to score more runs than your competition, make no errors, hit over 300, and win the pennant. Winning coaches set simple and clear targets that connect the vision to results.

Wright

How do "Profit-Driven Leaders" get people to do what they want them to do?

Hedley

Profit-driven leaders realize people who work for them are not the same as them. Your people don't think like you and they act different than you in every situation. And just because you pay them a good salary doesn't mean they're going to work their fanny off for you. You've got to give them a reason to want to follow your vision and achieve your goals. People are motivated for their reasons, not yours. Leaders don't get upset when people don't do things exactly the same way you do them with the same intensity. Younger workers today are different as well. They like continuous learning and growth. They want to participate in major decisions and they want balance in their life. Work may not be their number one priority. It is the leader's job to discover what makes each person tick and produce outstanding results.

For example, think of your children. You tell them what you want them to do, but they don't always do it. Then you try to bribe them— $100 for an "A," and they say, "Not enough, Dad." Frustrated, you scream, "If you're not home by 10:00 p.m., I'm gonna kill you!" Well, you don't. You let them off the hook. So they continue to stretch the envelope, as there was no accountability, no responsibility, and no consequences. It seems like nothing works with your kids, just like with your employees.

Leadership is really about influencing others to want to do what you want them to do. They key words are *"to want to do."* They've got to *want* to do it. You tell and they decide *if* they'll do it. When you tell your kids to clean up their room, they decide if they'll do it based on their needs, the consequences, accountabilities, and responsibilities which might affect their decision.

Ask yourself: "What makes people want to follow me?" You know what doesn't work (with your children and employees)—confusion, lack of trust, no integrity, no accountability, and no consequences. A lot of managers I meet in the business world say, "My people won't do what I want them to do. I should get rid of them, but I can't afford for them to leave, so I don't fire them." What kind of accountability is this? If they don't have to do what you want them to do, why should they do more than the minimum, to keep their job? You've got to make them want to do what you want them to do.

Realize people need two things—*money* & *happiness*. They need to get paid fairly, work for a secure company, and receive competitive benefits. Happiness is the same as being motivated. As an effective leader, your job is to motivate people to want to do what you want them to do. You accomplish this with inspirational leadership, continuous motivation, exciting vision, clear direction, holding people accountable, and giving them responsibility. The leader is responsible to encourage and motivate people to perform with energy, effort, and enthusiasm, so they'll go beyond where you want them to go.

Wright

Give us examples of how to get people to want to do what you want them to do?

Hedley

There are 4 action steps profit-driven leaders take to achieve bottom-line results through people. Number 1, the top priority is to provide clear expectations. People need to know exactly what you want them to achieve—the expected specific results. Weak leaders assume people understand what is required, don't take the time to spell out what they want, and then don't make their people account-able to get the results. The norm is to tell people to work real hard and try their best. But, this doesn't let people know exactly what's expected. People must be told and know exactly what you want, to get results: "By Friday, I expect you to have this installed and 100% com-plete." "By the 30th of the month all invoices must be out." Be specific with clear targets and exact results clearly defined. And, make sure your people understand what their target is, what's acceptable and what's not, when they hit or miss the target, the consequences for not achieving the results you want, and the rewards for a job well done.

The 2nd important action step leaders use to get the results they want is to provide ongoing recognition and praise to the people who do the work. Weak leaders don't take time to thank people for a job well done. This causes poor results. In a survey of why people left their company, over 90% said they'd never been recognized or praised by their boss, ever, for anything. People want and need feedback and positive reinforcement for their contributions and efforts. Profit-driven leaders give out praises at least every week to everyone in their sphere of influence. Use words like, "I appreciate you" and "Thanks for a great job."

The 3rd thing people need to do their best is a clear understanding of the big picture and how they fit in. Profit-driven leaders tell them where their company is going—its' vision, what the future has in store, positive and negatives, and the future changes required to be successful. People need to know; otherwise, they tend to think the worst. Several times a month I present seminars to company manag-ers who come up with great ideas to build and improve their businesses. When they go back to their offices the next day, their people are often afraid they've been scheming how to squeeze them to work harder. That's not reality, but without information people fear the worse. Profit-driven leaders constantly tell the real deal—business is good or bad, the future is positive or negative, sales are up or down, productivity is acceptable or not, our people are doing a good job or not.

The 4th action step profit-driven leaders do is to let their people know they care about them as individuals. People need to know you appreciate them; you care about their goals, their future, their kids, and their families. People must know they're important and their needs, wants, and desires will be addressed as they contribute to the entire organization's success.

Those are the four basic action steps required to lead people. There are lots of other things you can do to get your people to do what you want them to do. But, the main things are to tell them what you want, let them in on what's happening, recognize them, and show you care.

Wright

To get bottom-line results, what must "Profit-Driven Leaders" do first?

Hedley

Leadership is pretty simple. First, you've got to know exactly what _you_ want as a leader, for your company, your division, your department, or your project team. I speak to business owners and ask, "What do you want?" They respond, "I want to make a profit." I ask, "How much?" "As much as I can get." "What if you can't get very much?" "That's not enough." "Then how much do you want?" "More." "More than what?" "More than I'm getting now." They really don't know what they want.

Profit-driven leaders know exactly what they want. For example: "We want to make $100,000 net profit per month, per quarter, or per year." Specific. "We want our sales to be one million dollars per month with a net profit of $75,000 per month." "We want the project team to make $50,000 on this job and get at least 2 referrals from the customer." Leaders know what they want and communicate specific clear targets and deadlines for their people. And only then, can you develop a plan to get what you want. How can you ever build a plan to get _more_? More than what? Know what you want, have a plan, and then you can always make progress towards what you want.

Daily, you get pulled off track by day-to-day business activities. Things go wrong, customers or clients call with immediate needs, equipment breaks, or people don't show up. These daily inconveniences pull you off course and take you away from your number one priority, which may be bottom-line profit, sales, or customer service. You must have a written plan, keep on track, and measure your progress. I recommend written charts and graphs posted for all to see which clearly outline the progress toward the results you want.

Wright

How do "Profit-Driven Leaders" set clear targets and goals?

Hedley

Leaders have the right to set goals and targets based on what the company needs. According to *Fortune* magazine, a top quality of America's most admired companies is laser-like focus. They have a clear single business focus of what they're trying to do. For example: Wal-Mart—low prices, Nordstrom—customer service, GE—be number 1 or 2 in every business they undertake. In my opinion, that's not a path most small and medium business owners take. They try to do too much and be everything to everyone, instead of staying focused, doing what they do best, and only setting a few simple and attainable goals.

People and companies without clear written targets and goals, are used by those who have them. It's very interesting. Those who have written goals achieve them. Those who don't, get the leftovers. I always ask, "Have you got a measurable target? Do you have three clearly defined goals? What is your clear specific focus you want to achieve this year?" In a survey of over 2,000 business owners and managers I took, only 30% had written goals for sales, overhead, and profits. No wonder companies struggle!

Can you imagine playing golf on a new course without greens? It was built with one long fairway and the game was to keep hitting it down the middle. Score doesn't matter. After four hours, they blow a horn and you go into the bar and start drinking. There'd be no excitement. There's nothing to shoot for. There's no targets or scorecard. Sound bad? Sounds like most companies to me!

What are you really trying to accomplish? In order to get the results you want, you have to know exactly what you're shooting for and have a scorecard to keep track of your progress. You need information to be able to make adjustments as you go along. In golf, when you hit a bad shot, you are able to make the necessary adjustments to get back on course. In business, you've got different terrain and obstacles along the way to overcome. You need something to shoot at and a scorecard to keep track of your progress.

Wright

Can you explain why clear targets and specific goals are so important?

Hedley

Sure. You want to get everybody on the same page with a single pinpointed focus. Everybody in your organization needs clear targets and personal goals that fit into the overall business plan. They need something to shoot for and a scorecard to track their progress. As a contractor and business owner, it's often amazes me when I go out on to a jobsite and ask the field superintendent, "When are you going to get this part of the project completed?" He usually says, "Well, I think we'll get it done in a couple of months." I then ask, "How did you come up with that completion date?" He then says, "Well, I talked to the subcontractor's job foremen and we sort of agreed we could all get it done by then." I then ask, "Do you think you can finish it a week or two early?" He says, "Well, yeah, we probably could." "Why don't you?" "Well, there's no real need to. We're OK, we'll finish it on schedule." I say, "Wouldn't it be better to finish early?" "Yeah, but it doesn't really matter that much, does it?"

As a profit-driven leader, your job is to start challenging basic assumptions. You offer competitive challenges and encouragements like, "For every day you finish early on the project, I will give you $100. Do you think that might make a difference?" Then it's, "Oh yeah, I know we can finish at least a week early, maybe even more." So leaders know more incentives, more fun, specific challenging targets, and more communication get people focused to achieve the desired end results. When it's just the same old, same old, same old, people give you their minimum instead of their maximum. They go the easy comfortable route, rather than the exciting route where they make a difference and can be proud of their accomplishments. An effective leader spends time out with people keeping them on target and focused on getting better results than they think possible.

Wright

Do you have a simple system to set goals and targets?

Hedley

Yes, I created an acronym several years ago: "*SWAT.COM*." It's really simple. Goals need to be *Specific—S*. Goals must be very clear and specific. They can't be "finish as soon as you can." A clear goal might be "you must finish this project two weeks from Friday." They must be *Written—W*. If they're not written, they're not worth the paper they're not written on. When goals are written, they seem real and important. And, you can hold them up in front of your crew or team, and say, "Here's our goal. We're must get this finished by two weeks from Friday." *A—Attainable*. They can't be so difficult your people give up before they even get started. Set realistic goals to make your team work a little harder and get excited. *T—Time dependent*. They must have a really finite deadline. *C—Challenging & Clear*. People get excited about doing more than the ordinary or minimum required. Great goals challenge people to be and do their best. They also must be clearly understandable by all involved. If they can't repeat them and don't understand them, they'll never hit them. Goals must be *O—On-Target & On-Purpose* and in line with your company mission, vision, values, and what you stand for. A goal to make as much money as possible by cheating customers is probably not in line with your company philosophy. And finally, they've got to be *M—Measurable*. You must have a visible and measurable score-card—whether it's daily, weekly, monthly, quarterly, or annually. People need constant feedback and information to know if they're on track and making progress towards their goals.

One problem often happens when setting goals. If your goal, for example, is to finish a project on July 31st, and as the targeted completion date nears, you ask your manager, "Did you finish?" He says, "Yes, we're finished." You then walk the project and say, "You're not finished, there are still some small items to complete." And then you start arguing about what "finished" means. "Finished" may mean you've started the clean-up crews or maybe even turned over the project to your client. Or, it might mean 100% approved by the client or paid for in full. You've got to clearly define and make clear, specifically what was expected. Remember, the #1 key to getting results you want as a leader is clear expectations. Making sure your people clearly understand what was expected when you agreed on the words "done or finished."

Wright

How can "Profit-Driven Leaders" earn the trust of their people?

Hedley

Trust is an important requirement of leadership. Without trust, people won't follow you. Can you imagine buying products from a store or insurance from an agent you don't trust? You're just not going to do it. Would you vote for someone you don't trust?

For example, I'm out on a jobsite; I walk up to a cleanup crew laborer and ask, "Why aren't you using the wheelbarrow to help you get the job done faster?" He says, "My foreman wasn't here this morning and he didn't give me the key to the storage bin. So I'm just using a shovel to carry the trash across the jobsite to the trash container." I now think: "Boy is this situation stupid! Why doesn't he trust you with the key?"

People, who aren't trusted, don't go the extra mile. They just go through the motions and only do the minimum. The leader's goal is to develop and encourage trust. Rather than doing the important jobs for your people, and keeping them in the dark when it comes to decisions, you've got to trust your people to be and do their best. In a Gallop survey poll, 66% of workers were asked to make decisions, but only 14% said that they'd been empowered and trusted to make decisions. A bad example of leadership is at hotels where there's a little card on the table that says, "For immediate response to any concern, this form is addressed to the president of the hotel." The president's office is 2,000 miles away. He obviously doesn't trust his people to take care of their needs. Put people in charge; give them the tools, responsibility, and the authority. Then watch them make great decisions and a HUGE difference.

Do people ever line up outside your office door waiting for you to solve their problems? Why is that? Maybe you have a sign around your neck that says, "ISOPP" (I solve other people's problems). As a high school student I completed a career aptitude survey. I was really proud when I found out I'm a person who likes to solve problems. But this became a problem for me as a business owner. When I solved other people's problems, guess what happens? They bring me more problems! People know when they make decisions, their boss tends to second-guess them and often overrules. Bad bosses don't trust people to be as smart as them. So people stop making decisions, stop being responsible, give back accountability, and continue to bring you more problems. People responsible for nothing are responsible for nothing; and 99% responsible is the same as 0% responsible. Either you are responsible or you're not. You can't be partially responsible. Bosses can't say, "Handle this, but check with me first." Trusting people is the key to improving their performance.

I had a stamp designed I use when people give me a written request for my approval. It states, *"Please handle this and don't tell me what you did!"* Why? Because I don't want to know how they handled the problem they want me to solve for them! I trust them to use their best judgment and take care of it. People will make mistakes. But, when you ask them to be 100% accountable and responsible, they'll figure out how to do it right and make good careful decisions. If you continually answer their questions and do their job for them, they're going to keep asking you for more help.

So, whom can you trust? Leadership is not about control. It's about delegating, encouraging, coaching, and letting go. It's about low control. Low control equals high performance. High control equals low performance. The more you let go of, the more time you have to do what really matters. The more you coach, empower, and encourage, the more leadership opportunities you'll have. People want to follow people who make them accountable and responsible, and then let them do the work and get results. A leader's role is less about what he can do and more about what his people and his team can do.

One of your primary leadership roles is to inspire others to become the best they can be. Not tell, not do, but inspire. I've had to change my role in my company over the last 20 years, from a hands-on control freak to an inspirer, encourager, motivator, and coach to get the results I want. And this now makes me real excited about coming to work. In my speaking presentations, I ask business owners and managers on their handouts to draw a circle the size of a quarter. Then, I ask them to write all the things in that circle they can't let go of or delegate. In my opinion, there's really nothing you can't let go of or delegate except mission, vision, values, and setting clear "SWAT.COM" goals and targets. Everything else can be delegated with enough staff and resources. Obviously smaller business owners and managers can't let go of everything they do, but they could delegate at least 50% of what they do right now, especially if they have a few people working for them. What will you let go of to trust and empower your people to be the best they can be? The more you don't do, the more you will make happen.

Wright

To get results through people, what else can a leader do?

Hedley

Profit-driven leaders realize getting results starts at the top, with the leader. (The top can be a project team leader, foreman, division manager, or anyone who is responsible to get results through people.) Results are the main indicator of a leader. The results people produce is the number one reflection of the leader's ability to lead. Making a positive difference and getting people to change starts with the leader. When someone comes to you with a problem, encourage him or her to come back with answers rather than fix it for them. If things aren't going well, leaders realize they must be the first to change and change how they lead. You've got to try something new. Leaders lead by doing. For example, they must be the first person to try new ideas or systems like computerization or new company procedures.

Change, innovation, growth, and improvement, starts with the leader—not their employees. A way to improve your leadership performance is to ask, "What do I have to do differently, to get different results?" Remember, one of your jobs is to improve other people's performance, not demand it. I'm always asking myself, "How can I help other people improve? Who's becoming a leader because of me? Who has potential and needs encouragement?" My job is to help people achieve the results we both want.

People want to be accountable and responsible. Poor leaders don't give it away and control from their position of authority. Most people want to do more and be the best they can be. Remember when you first came to work for your company? You were excited. After about three weeks, you got disenchanted as your boss didn't give you opportunities, didn't trust you, and didn't encourage you. It became just another lousy job. Your number one priority became finding a better job. Leaders don't let this happen in their organizations.

Profit-driven leaders ask, "How can I get my people more motivated to follow me?" It may be through challenges, feedback, mentoring, coaching, encouragement, motivation, continuous learning, personal growth, or self-development. Ask yourself, "Am I getting the results I want from my people? How many business and leadership books or magazines have I read this year? When was the last time I went to a leadership seminar or workshop? Am I investing in my future? Am I changing and keeping up with the times and new business and leadership ideas, or am I stuck in the past?" Leaders often want their people to change and improve without fixing themselves first. Do you go to work, see the same people, the same suppliers, and the same customers, year after year, expecting different and better bottom-line results? Do you try the same leadership techniques ten years in a row expecting to make more money? Look in the mirror. Your leadership challenge might start with you!

Being a profit-driven leader starts with a HUGE passion for getting results. Inspire people to go higher than they can imagine. Try new ideas and take the first step necessary to make it happen. Get excited about the future. Embrace change and make it part of your every day actions. Love people and realize they are the only resource you have that matters. Spend at least half of your time out with your people encouraging, motivating, recognizing, providing feedback, checking progress on targets, and helping people become the best they can be. Profit-driven leaders get the results they want. Are you a profit-driven leader?

Wright

What a great conversation. I really want to tell you how much I appreciate you spending this much time with me today on this really interesting topic.

Hedley

Thank you.

Wright

Today we have been talking to George Hedley, Certified Speaking Professional and entrepreneur. He is the recognized expert on growing a successful business and known in many circles as the "Profit-Builder." George, thank you so much for being with us on *Conversations on Leadership*.

Hedley

Thank you and you're welcome. It's been **HUGE**!

George Hedley, CSP the "Profit-Builder" is the recognized expert on growing a successful business. He founded and built his $75 million dollar construction and development company and received the nationally recognized "Entrepreneur of the Year" award. Today, along with managing his company, he owns HARDHAT Presentations helping business owners always make a profit, develop leaders, create loyal customers, build wealth, and get their businesses to work. He is the author of *On-Purpose...On-Target!* and *Everything Contractors Know About Making A Profit.*

George Hedley

HARDHAT Presentations

3189-B Airway Avenue

Costa Mesa, California 92626

Phone: 714.437.1122

Toll Free: 800.851.8553

Email: gh@hardhatpresentations.com

www.hardhatpresentations.com

Chapter 12

PHILIP RESCH

THE INTERVIEW

David E. Wright (Wright)

Today we're talking to Philip Resch. He has more than 30 years of experience as a business leader in operations and human resources. He is currently a Partner with the retained executive search firm Sandhurst Group. As Senior Vice President of Operations for the Pacific Maritime Association (PMA), he led operations and was a member of the executive committee, trustee on the Health and Welfare plans, and one of the chief negotiators for the contract with International Longshore and Warehouse Union (ILWU). As Senior Vice President, Worldwide for Fujitsu-ICL Retail Systems, he played a significant role in the movement of the worldwide retail division to Dallas, Texas, positioning Fujitsu as the leader in the retail and financial industries. Previous positions include Vice President of Human Resources and Administration for Greenwich Air Services, formerly the largest independent aircraft parts services company in the world, and Director of Human Resources for Ryder Systems and the Ford Motor Company. After graduating from the University of Louisville on an NROTC scholarship, Phil served as a Surface Warfare Officer in the Navy. He received his Masters in Business Management from Webster University and has a Juris Doctorate degree from the Brandeis School of Law University of Louisville. He recently retired as a Captain in the Naval Reserve. Phil Resch, welcome to *Conversations on Leadership*! In your opinion, what are the critical traits and skills of a leader?

Philip Resch (Resch)

Well, David, I really think that there are several critical traits and skills that leader's must have. The first of these is to "become yourself." Second, they must have vision. Third, they must have self-motivation. All of these critical traits and skills must have a solid underpinning of values. These values are honor, courage, commitment, and of course they must have enthusiasm.

Wright

What is becoming yourself?

Resch

Becoming yourself is the core of who you are. It's not about being someone else; it's the sum of who you are and what you stand for. It is the essence of your authentic self, your values, your belief system, your thoughts and actions. Becoming yourself is knowing what is important to you. It is knowing when to dig deep and give your all. Warren Bennis, in his book On Becoming a Leader, talked about leaders knowing themselves thoroughly before they can hope to lead others.

Becoming yourself is a very important stop and step on the way to becoming a leader and achieving success. Becoming yourself is difficult to achieve; it's a lifetime learning and unlearning process. Just about the time you think you have become yourself something happens in your life to alter your course. You experience marriage, birth of your child, a divorce, death of a loved one or a serious medical problem. These all alter your path and they all test you. In life you are going to have setbacks. You are going to have adversities, sorrows along with successes. It's when something like this comes to test you that you turn to introspection. You learn to dig deep and draw upon your life's experiences. You draw upon yourself. How you respond to these events is up to you. Your response tests who you are and this develops you. There's an old saying that if you haven't failed at something you're not really trying. It has some merit here. We all get scars and get beat up at times. It's how we handle both setbacks and successes that we truly grow as an individual. Paul Bear Bryant said it:

"The first time you quit it's hard; the second time you quit it gets easier; that third time you do it, you don't even have to think about it."

Part of becoming yourself is that ability not to quit, an ability to handle adversity and change. Change is the only constant thing in a leader's life. Change is something that has become a constant. That may sound like an oxymoron, but the good old days are right now. You can't go back. A leader has to be adaptable and has to have the ability to look at change and shape his or herself around it. Those who fear change will have a difficult time truly becoming themselves and thus will not fully develop as a leader. People follow leaders and leaders handle change. Navy Admiral and business leader, Sonny Masso is fond of saying, "If you always do what you always did you'll always get what you always got." The translation of this means you have to be adaptable. You have to embrace change. On the way to becoming yourself and becoming a leader you have to reevaluate yourself and reevaluate everything around you and adapt to that change or difference. You must always be doing that 360° recon, looking around and observing what's going on. Leaders have to be able to influence others to follow them and you cannot influence until you become yourself. A good leader also is a good follower and provides feedback support and follows their leader.

Wright

So, you're suggesting that this is continuing introspection.

Resch

Absolutely, it's a lifelong process. Leadership develops daily and not in a day. About the time you think you've got it down, believe me, something happens in your life that just turns it upside down, such as a change at work—change of a boss or a company is purchased or merged and you have to think about how you're going to handle this. You have to dig deep upon who you. Leaders are able to do that.

Wright

What do you mean by vision, and is vision different from goals?

Resch

Vision is the leader's ability to see beyond just today. A good leader sees beyond what's going on at the very moment. In other words, vision is knowing where you want to be and a strategy is how you are going to get there. As a naval officer, I learned many things about leadership. The Navy deploys ships and they have to sail from one destination to another. For 98% of that voyage you can not see the destination, yet somehow the ships made it to the right port. But how does this happen? In the old days we steered by the sun and stars and employed dead reckoning. Today, we've got the satellites and GPS to help us. These were the tools to get us there, but what got you heading to the right port was a plan—a vision of our mission and where we wanted to go. David, if I kidnapped you and dropped you off where you had no idea where you were and I instructed you to go to Dallas, Texas, how in the heck would you get there? To assist you, I will even provide you with a map. Not knowing where you are, a map would be useless. Leaders know where they are at all times. Leaders know where they want to go. If you don't know who you are and where you are, you're going to have a difficult time as a leader to be able to lead people.

George Patton is an excellent example of a leader. Throughout World War II he had a truck that he took to the front lines so he could be with his men and lead from the front. In the truck there was a large map of the operating area, including his goal, Berlin. Patton also had studied the area and had traveled extensively after World War I throughout France and Germany. He always knew where he wanted to go and he was able to quickly adapt and change directions because he knew where he and his troops were at the moment. It is imperative for a leader to have this type of vision.

I also think a leader needs to have vision in their spiritual and personal life. It is foolish just to have vision in your business life. An effective leader has a balance and a clear vision in all three of these areas. A successful leader is well balanced. A leader must also have a clearly developed strategy to follow the developed vision. Armed with a vision and the strategy to execute the vision, a leader is not stopped when something blocks the way. An effective leader has developed vision to draw from which allows a leader to find a way around the obstacle or even use the obstacle as an advantage. David, a vision has some similarity to a goal, but I think it's more encompassing. Goals have a finished, defined objective while a vision is a lot more fluid. You can define a goal as a destination, but a vision is more. It is the journey to that destination. In setting a vision, leaders are able to set priorities. Everything can't be an "A," although my life seems to be full of "A's" lately. A leader develops their vision and balances that vision with what is at hand. A leader can change and adapt a strategy to fit what's required to accomplish their vision. The military action in the War with Iraq is a good example of how a plan with a vision became adaptable. As the weather turned and the enemy collapsed, the leaders were able to adapt and change the timetables and directions and head directly for the capital city and quickly bring an end to the military portion in the war with Iraq.

Wright

What is self-motivation and self-discipline?

Resch

I think self-motivation is not motivation; it's certainly something a little bit different. Self-motivation comes from within as where motivation may not come from within; it may come from what's outside. Growing up in Louisville I got to meet Paul Horning, the Heisman Trophy winner from Notre Dame and the all-pro football player for the Green Bay Packers. We were fortunate to share the same High School Football coach whose style was like Vince Lombardi's. Once, in a conversation with Paul I made the statement, "It must have been great to play with a coach like Vince Lombardi, someone who can motivate you to greatness." Paul looked at me with a laugh and said, "You think Lombari could motivate me, or Jim Taylor or Max McGee or Fuzzy Thurston? No, he couldn't, but he provided an environment where we could be self-motivated." I learned from this that a leader provides the environment where others can be self-motivated. I think this is a very important point.

Trying to motivate others to do things is not that easy. A test for this is if you have kids. It is tough to motivate them, they have their agendas. But, you can provide an environment where they can be self motivated and self-disciplined. No one can tell you to get up in the morning. The late basketball coach Jim Valvano said, "You just have to get yourself jacked up, juiced up, and ready to go." This takes discipline. When we talk about discipline we do not mean it from the punitive sense. I was fortunate to work for an impressive leader, Navy Admiral Tim Jenkins. Tim taught us that you must be self-disciplined as a leader. He stressed habits—training and doing things right. He also stressed that leaders recognize those who do a good job. Leaders need to provide the environment for their followers to be self-disciplined. Leaders themselves must always set the example and be self-disciplined and self-motivated. To accomplish this, effective leaders must develop good habits and solid values. A leader is able to communicate these, and constantly lead by setting an example.

Wright

I have heard that there are only two kinds of pain in life—the pain of discipline or the pain of regret. I've often thought of that and I think you just said it in another way. Why are values so important?

Resch

Values are the principles or qualities that guide your life and decisions. The alignment of what you say and what you do is important to the success of a leader. I am often asked where you get these values. Hopefully you get a solid foundation while you're growing up. During my grade school and high school years I was surrounded by a tremendous group of people—my classmates and their families became an extended family. It was "Yes, sir" and "No, ma'am." When one of the parents spoke it was as if our own parent had said something to us and we certainly obeyed. This created an environment of trust and respect. This coupled with the values from my parents allowed me to understand what I stood for. It's important to understand who you are. It's important for a successful leader to have a good set of values that he or she can draw from. A successful leader draws on these values as they need them and they become a foundation—a foundation for a leader to stand on. There are few examples in history of individuals who lead and lacked solid values. These leaders eventually failed those that they led. Who you are and what you stand for states volumes about you. The foundation of what you believe in is very important. Successful leaders will put everything on the line to stay with their values. Once you've compromised your values you've compromised your ability to be a successful leader.

Wright

Can you share with our readers some of the values and characteristics that a leader should exhibit?

Resch

I sure can. Honor, courage, and commitment, were some of the core values that I grew up with and were ingrained in me while I was in the Navy. Enthusiasm is also something that a leader needs. By honor, I mean the integrity, the responsibility, the accountability of how a leader conducts him or herself. With honor we conduct ourselves in the highest ethical manners in relationships with everyone around us. It's critical that a leader demonstrate that. You must be honest, you have to be truthful, you must have honor in dealing with yourself and your dealings with other people.

A successful leader has got to be willing to make honest recommendations and accept recommendations from others. This means a good leader is comfortable in their own skin. Comfortable in their own skin is another way of saying that they have become themselves. A successful leader will encourage new ideas and at the same time have to be able to deliver the bad news. An effective leader has to be able to receive bad news without killing the messenger. Sometimes, it's very unpopular and it's tough to deliver bad news. They'll have the ability to abide by an uncompromising code of integrity. A good leader has the honor and integrity to fulfill and exceed their legal and ethical responsibilities all around them. This is a 24-hour a day thing; this is not just an occasional thing. Honor also means there will be no illegal, improper behavior. Even the appearance of such behavior is not tolerable. We're accountable for our professional and personal behavior. Lately there have been many striking examples of companies and individuals not conducting themselves with honor. These people failed as leaders and they failed their organization. The scandals at Enron, WorldCom, and other companies stem from the inability of people to be honorable in their dealings with people within and outside the corporation. The leaders failed because they didn't show the integrity that they needed. Leaders must have a sense of responsibility. This is arguably one of the most important traits of a successful leader. A professional leadership expert and friend of mine, Barry Benator says, "If the leader is not responsible nothing else matters because little else is going to happen." With that responsibility goes accountability. A leader is accountable for their actions or their inactions.

By courage, I mean a leader must do the right thing in the right way and has to make decisions for the right reasons. This courage is a value that gives us moral and mental strength to do what's right even in the face of personal or professional adversity. Growing up in Louisville, we had a neighbor Pee Wee Reese, the baseball hall of famer and former captain of the professional baseball team the Brooklyn Dodgers. Pee Wee provided guidance to our family after our parents died. He taught us a lot. One of the things that I remember about Pee Wee was his courage. When Jackie Robinson was brought in to play professional baseball, there were many people who did not want an African American to play in the big leagues. Pee Wee thought otherwise and he put his career on the line and took a leadership position.

He stated he was going to play ball with Jackie and if the rest of the team was not, he was ashamed of being their captain. He then led the team onto the field and put his arm around Jackie, right out there in the middle of the field by second base, and confirmed to all the team, all the fans, all the naysayers that he was going to stand by him as a friend. Jackie and Pee Wee became lifelong friends. Pee Wee had the courage to put it all on the line and make a difference. He did this because of his values and he knew that it was in the best interest of his profession and team. He demonstrated loyalty and he demonstrated great judgment in how he handled the situation. Courage, like the type that Pee Wee demonstrated has impact on followers. People follow leaders. They follow people who demonstrate great courage and people who make tough decisions. It's difficult to have the courage to make a tough decision. Many fail in leadership and are not successful because they don't have the courage to do what's right.

Commitment is another important value. Commitment is a leader being able to live up to a pledge or promise, or to obligate themselves to the cause or endeavor that they're in. The leader must demand and show respect to everyone and is committed to positive change and constant improvement. By a leader exhibiting this high degree of moral character they can be successful. An example of a leader making a commitment can be demonstrated by Margaret Thatcher who when the rest of Europe toyed with socialism and state ownership, she set about privatizing the nationalized industries. This was very unpopular and she risked her political career. She made the tough decisions that resulted in a stronger Britain and much of Europe following her example.

Another important value is enthusiasm. Enthusiasm is a synonym for the word passion. It comes from the Greek word to be inspired. I don't think you can be successful as a leader unless you have enthusiasm. Ralph Waldo Emerson said, "Nothing great was ever achieved without some enthusiasm." I will personally take an enthusiastic leader over one who is less inspired.

Wright

Why is it important to build a foundation?

Resch

A foundation is the base that a leader builds upon. It's important to build a solid foundation and keep building on it throughout your life. I had a great uncle who was in the Barnum and Bailey Circus. I remember visiting him when we were young and he talked about being in the circus and working under the big top. Years later, as I watched a large tent being erected it reminded me of his stories of the circus tents. Watching them erecting the tents, they had to put the long poles up first. Once the long poles were in place this laid the foundation for putting up the rest of the tent. Without the poles in place, the tent could not be erected. Once the poles were in there the tent seemed to rise in an instant around these poles. This is what I mean by building that solid foundation. You have to set up the long poles first: the foundation. A leader needs to build a foundation on their values. A leader then needs to work on building the characteristics required to be a leader; becoming yourself, vision and self-motivation. A solid foundation must be laid so a leader can draw from it when required. A leader then, has to be able to learn, but as important to un-learn. Only when this is incorporated in your foundation will you be able to change. Your ability to change equates to your ability to become a leader. Foundation is an important building block in leadership.

Wright

If a person works on all of these characteristics that you've just mentioned, and traits, will they be successful?

Resch

Again, there's no magic in becoming a leader. It takes a lot of hard work. It takes some opportunity. I don't think you can go around and create a circumstance for you to lead, but you might be able to lead when the circumstance presents itself. To do this you must have grasped the importance of what we're talking about in this book *Conversations on Leadership*. Success could be a relative term to some. Without becoming philosophical, success is all in the eye of how you see it. When I was 25, I was convinced I was the smartest person in the world and that I was an effective leader. One season I learned a valuable leadership lesson. I had the experience of working with a man who helped me coach my daughter's softball team. He was a World War II and Korean War veteran. He was in the UDT (Underwater Demolition teams). When I first met him I could not understand why he was not a CEO of a company. Instead of climbing the corporate ladder, he chose to have a job that allowed him to spend quality time with his family and to give back to the community and his church. He had made the decision to place his leadership and energy in this direction. This allowed him to have an impact on many of those around him. I learned that he was a very successful man and a leader; he had followers, including me. During that season I learned a lot from him. It was not until years later that I realized he had it right. He had built a solid foundation of values. He had the perspective and vision of what he wanted to do in life and what he wanted to become. He was comfortable in his own skin; he had become himself. He was a leader and everyone around him knew it. Working with this man and the team helped me develop as a leader.

Another lesson that I learned, was that leaders sometimes sit back and do not always have to be in the front lines or in the front of an organization to be effective. Sometimes an effective leader can be someone that's not playing a major role, but somebody who's leading from the back and directing and adding value and influencing. In today's fast-paced world people are learning to make choices. They are learning it's important to make choices. They are learning that what is important to them is valuable and that they can have balance in their spiritual, personal and business life and still be an effective leader.

Wright

Can anyone become a leader?

Resch

John Maxwell once said, "It's not the position that makes a leader; it's the leader that makes the position." You can learn to become a leader. To be an effective leader you have to be a good learner, but more importantly as I stated earlier, you have to be a good unlearner. It took a long time for me to understand that you have to unlearn some things. One of the more difficult lessons I learned in consulting and advising senior leadership is to inform those people in the positions that they really are not being successful because they haven't learned new ways. You have to teach them to un-learn. Even if you are successful, to continue to be a good leader you're going to have to unlearn some things and you're going to have to learn some new things. Everyone has the opportunity to become a leader, but some do not have the burning desire nor have they laid the foundation to become an effective leader. To become a leader you're going to have to embrace some of the expertise shared in this book, *Conversations on Leadership*. You're going to have to be able to become yourself, have a solid vision, make sure you understand your values, and be able to pull all this together. I think if you do all that you will be well on your way to becoming a leader. Remember, not everyone wants to become a leader. Not everyone wants to assume that type of responsibility. Some people are comfortable to be followers. Remember, there is a great need for loyal followers as well.

Wright

Someone told me many years ago in a leadership course, "David, if you think you're a leader and you look around and no one's following you, then you're only out for a walk." I guess what he was trying to say is that leadership is delegated from the bottom. The people who follow you will determine whether or not you're a leader.

Resch

David, that is exactly on point. If you do not have followers then you will not be an effective leader. Warren Bennis and Burt Nanus stated that the capacity to develop and improve their skills is what distinguished leaders from followers. So, if there are no followers it is impossible to lead.

Wright

Do you have any examples of a leader? Is a leader the same thing as a role model?

Resch

I think there's a little bit of difference between a role model and a leader. You can be a role model and be a leader and you can be a role model and not be a leader. I do have some examples. It is important to remember that following or having a role model doesn't mean that you want to become that person. I think sometimes people go too far in trying to be their role model or they are trying to keep up with the Jones's. I was lucky; I had several role models growing up. One we talked about earlier was Pee Wee Reese. He demonstrated and taught us how important it was to have values, how important it was to stand for something that you believed in, no matter how unpopular it was. He taught us to "hang tough." That was his favorite saying. He'd say to us, "Come on boys, and hang tough."

There was another guy who was about eight years older that I looked to as a role model. My parents said when I was about seven I made the announcement that I wanted to become a Captain in the Navy. I guess I had an early vision, because I was able to do that. It was interesting that my role model also wanted to be a jet pilot. He did that by joining the Air National Guard and later became a successful airline pilot. He was a good role model. He was a top athlete and a good student. I watched him attain his vision and I followed my vision using him as a role model. So it is great to have a role model.

Also, growing up, I read a lot of autobiographies. I read about Daniel Boone, Theodore Roosevelt, George Rogers Clark and others. Theodore Roosevelt was a leader. Here was a guy who grew up very sickly, but built himself up physically and mentally. He studied to become the person he wanted to be. He had tremendous impact in every position he was ever in—Secretary of the Navy, Lieutenant Colonel leading his men up San Juan Hill, Medal of Honor recipient and President of our country. He was a leader—whether he was leading people in world events or in environmental concerns. As Americans we have a lot to thank him for, especially his vision as a leader to open up some of the US lands as National Parks.

George Patton is another example of an extraordinary leader. He had tremendous vision. He knew from an early age that he wanted to lead men into battle. He knew he wanted to be a general so he started acting like a general. He did this from the time he was a very young army officer despite his dyslexia. He started studying everything he could possibly study on leaders, war and general leadership subjects. He earned the respect of his men. He had to set up the disciplined environment we talked about earlier. He understood that he had to have a vision of where he wanted to go. He had to be able at all times to set an example and be that general. He had an image of what he thought a general should be. He acted like he thought a general would. He had a lot of followers, and people who did follow him to the ultimate end.

Another example of a leader is someone we talked about earlier, Vince Lombardi. Lombardi provided those environments where people could exceed and excel. He had a lot of faith in his assistant coaches. A lot of his assistant coaches went on to become great coaches in their own right. He influenced the team and his team members followed him to glory.

In the business world, Jack Welch, the former chairman of General Electric was an effective leader. He produced a culture were he lead the entire executive team to un-learn some of the very things that had made General Electric successful. He reinvented the entire company to where only a small portion of the company today is in the businesses it was when he took the helm. He led General Electric to be one of the most effective companies in the world. George Bush '41 is another good example of a leader—someone who stood by and had to make some really tough decisions in the first Gulf War. He had to decide that this was the right thing to do. He knew it was the right thing to do for the world at the time, but he pushed ahead. Even though it was unpopular he knew that he had to go forward and do this. Leaders take risks. Those are just some examples of some individuals who are great leaders.

Wright

I was talking to Jim Tunney recently, who was a good friend of Coach Lombardi's, and he reminded me that of all of the things that made him great. When I asked what he thought was the greatest attribute he said it was his faith. Lombardi was a man of faith. He said he went to church every single day. Then, Jim told me that Paul Horning told him that he went to church every day because of some of the things he did on the field.

Resch

Faith and a strong spiritual life are important to a leader. I think that there are a lot of people out there who miss this connection. They are not comfortable with themselves and have not been able to give themselves up to someone else who is on a lot higher order then they are. Strong spiritual beliefs and faith seem to have a powerful impact on leaders. Those who use them appear to be much more effective as leaders. It is interesting to notice that those leaders we talked about above all had faith and a strong spiritual life as a common factor. Sometimes it's the people who work for you that make you a good leader. As we said earlier, you have to be able to adapt and rise to the occasion. You have to lead a Paul Horning differently than you'd lead someone like a Jim Tunney, one of the great referees out there. You have to understand where your followers are so you can decide the best way to lead them. You have to lead people a little differently. You have to adapt. A leader has that ability to see, sense and adapt to the situation. They do this using skill sets developed from a solid foundation. Effective leaders have intuitive skills. That is the intuition of what to do, a feel for what is required. Skills like that, becoming yourself and vision along with solid values come from experience.

Wright

What a great conversation, Phil. I've learned a lot here today. I certainly want to thank you for spending so much time with me and answering the questions that I had. Today we've been talking to Philip Resch. He has had more than 30 years of experience as a business leader in operations and human resources. He's recently retired as a Captain in the naval reserve and we hope will be training on leadership for days and years to come. Phil, thank you for being with me on *Conversations on Leadership*.

Resch

Thank you, David.

About The Author

Philip Resch has 30 years business leader experience in operations and HR. Currently Partner with the Sandhurst Group Executive Search. Previous: SVP Operations Pacific Maritime Association , SVP Worldwide for Fujitsu-ICL Retail Systems, VP HR & Administration Greenwich Air Services, Director HR Ryder Systems and the Ford Motor Company. BA University of Louisville; Masters Business Management Webster University; Juris Doctorate Brandeis School of Law University of Louisville. Recently retired as a Captain in the Naval Reserve.

Philip Resch
Sandhurst Group
8214 Westchester Suite 500
Dallas, Texas 75225
Phone: 972.769.1053
www.Sandhurstgroup.com

Chapter 13

TONI L. DUVAL

THE INTERVIEW

David E. Wright (Wright)

Today we are talking to Toni Duval. She is founder and president of TLD-Training and Leadership Development, which was established in 1994. TLD is a full service training and skill development consulting firm capable of creating and facilitating a wide variety of training programs including leadership and team building events, retreats, workshops, and other special learning activities. Ms. Duval has been in the training and development field for 22 years, and her passion and energy underlie the value TLD delivers to its clients. Ms. Duval and TLD have succeeded at partnering with major corporations including ALSTOM, Saturn Motors, Nashville Electric Service, and Tennessee Minority Supplier Development Council following her careers at Commonwealth Mortgage Company, State Savings Bank, and Travelers Insurance Corporation. Ms. Duval has developed many unique seminars and training tools for leadership and professional development. She is a graduate of the University of Connecticut and obtained advanced learning at Radcliffe College's Advanced Management Program along with numerous corporate training programs. Toni, welcome to *Conversations on Leadership*.

Toni Duval (Duval)
Thanks, David. It's great to be here.

Wright
Few people approach their work with such enthusiasm and high energy. Have you always been this energetic?

Duval
Yes, I was literally born with optimism. I was a premature baby, born seven weeks early, and in the 1950's there was more doubt than hope for the survival of a three and a half pound baby. But to this day, I believe my strong will and determination plus my anticipation of the joys that life would bring pulled me through those weeks in the hospital. You know, David, I've never been sick since then.

Wright
How about that!

Duval
Yes, in fact, since I've been old enough to understand the implications of my birth, my perspective has been, "Why would I go through all the trouble to arrive on the planet early just to leave?" Once here, I was here to stay. I've lived each day of my life this way. When I decided to start my business in 1994, I was driven by a vision of how TLD could impact the lives of others. Driven by optimism that the vision would work, I approached each day enthusiastically about its possibilities. Almost a decade later, I'm proud of TLD's accomplishments.

Wright
I understand that both your parents were in the education industry. How do you think having two parents in academia influenced your career choices?

Duval
Yes, both of my parents were educators. Like many of their peers, they reaped the early benefits of the Civil Rights Movement. My mother, Billie, who was originally from a coal-mining town in southwest Virginia, met my father while she was in college. My dad, Sonny, had returned to college after the Korean War. They both worked in the Hartford, Connecticut school system after they were

married. They retired in 1983. My mom was a long time physical education teacher and high school vice-principal. My dad was a guidance counselor and school administrator. To say that I learned a lot from them, is an understatement. They were both, and still are to this day, highly opinionated, independent, and competitive individuals. Even though back in my day they held very high standards for behavior, they both actively encouraged me to explore all my options and challenge the status quo as well as to seek to understand the perspectives of other people. So you'd think that my choice to be an educator of sorts would have been an easy one, but being their daughter, I had to explore all my options. My parents are avid golfers, David, yet, I am a long distance swimmer. They liked jazz and I like jazz too, but I like bluegrass as well. They would just as soon go to a spa, and my idea of a vacation is 18 days on a raft on the Colorado River in the Grand Canyon. So, it didn't seem like much of a surprise to them that after five years of college and a degree in Mass Communications, I decided to become a waitress. But eventually, in 1986, I took on a special project that involved creating a training department for a New England based mortgage company. After about 90 days, I had to call my mother and tell her that I had found my calling. Even though it wasn't exactly teaching in the traditional sense, it was facilitating learning in the workplace and I just loved it.

Wright

I gather then that since your business is leadership development, you believe that leadership is a skill that can be developed.

Duval

You know, David, if you believe that leaders are only born, then you limit your access to the talent pool out there, and you limit the capacity of your team, or your organization, or even of a nation. To me that's not really the American way. I believe that if a person has the willingness and the desire to improve his or her performance, and he or she is given the opportunities and the tools to succeed, then even though one might not be the best in every aspect of one's job, that person will be better off than where they started. Leadership is like any other work competency. It is a set of knowledge, skills, and abilities that can be observed, measured, and developed. Just think of it, for years people believed that black men and women could never lead and motivate white men and women. Additionally, there was a notion that women couldn't be decisive enough to lead large companies.

However, no matter what your political affiliation or area of expertise, you must agree that these myths and many more were exposed only after opportunities were extended and people stepped up to the challenge. I believe that one of the American workforce's best assets is our ability to step up to the challenge and preparing today's workforce to do this is a key to leadership.

Wright

For our readers, could you describe your core concept of leadership?

Duval

I'd be glad to. I like to apply the saying, "Think globally, act locally!" to leadership. Everyone agrees that it's the leader's role to understand the vision, stick to the mission, set the course, and steer the ship. But to do that, you have to impact each person every day. We have to build relationships and share experiences during the every day moments of our day-to-day lives. Then during crunch time, people will choose the correct thing to do. They will be empowered as leaders as well. When I was hired by a growing savings bank in Salem, Massachusetts, the newly hired president, Bill Mitchellson, made a point of hiring six or seven young people. Some, like me, had no financial experience or background. He believed that as rookies, we would see things differently. We were expected to ask questions. We were expected to form opinions. We were expected to look for ways to improve policies and procedures. Throughout my time there, Bill made a point to stop by the branch or whatever department we happened to be in to sit down and chat. He used to hold "gab fests," as he called them, where he asked us and other employees to share our opinions and make suggestions. He really listened to what we had to say. His management style became the benchmark for my career, and to this day, I continue to evaluate leaders by their ability to set the course, empower their workforce to meet challenges along the way, and listen with openness to others' opinions.

Wright

Is leadership a profession, or do you believe it's a lifestyle?

Duval

I'd have to agree with leadership guru John Maxwell who says, "The position does not make the leader, the leader makes the position." Regardless of your position, you can practice leadership in your day-to-day activities. You can extend your reach and increase your influence. However, you can't do that if you're closed off from your team or your organization. In the mailroom, there's a leader that has saved the company thousands of dollars in shipping costs. In accounting, there's a leader who daily places the interests of the company over her own individual needs or desires. As leaders, it's up to us to actively pursue these individuals. In addition, leadership is dynamic, and one's ability to lead is often measured by his or her ability to also be a part of the team. I believe in shared leadership both on the job and in life. I guess my answer would be, that leadership isn't something you can take on or off like a suit or a pair of shoes. It's a way of life.

Wright

Often leadership messages are easy to understand, but difficult to put into practice. How do your workshops enable people to put your principles into practice?

Duval

At TLD, we employ what we call the three "E"s. Like our mission says, our learning events are enlightening, empowering, and enjoyable. Participants create action plans to achieve their own learning objectives. This is the enlightening part. Everyone, including the facilitator, learns at least one new thing. That's our quality guarantee. Secondly, we empower the learners with tools and methods to improve their performance. We break down behaviors into skill-based learning modules. We also use self-assessment, observation, and other tools to evaluate success and provide feedback. With almost 20 years of professional training under my belt, though, there is one thing I know for sure, and that's adults learn better if they are enjoying the process. We develop elaborate activities and encourage the use of toys and games. When comfortable and in a give-and-take environment, adults are more likely to participate in their own learning process, and that's the environment we like to establish.

Wright

Will you share with us your company's approach or philosophy about how adults learn to adjust and modify their current behavior in order to develop new skills?

Duval

Sure. I believe one of the strengths of TLD learning events, whether they are workshops, special off-site retreats, conference activities, or even facilitative meetings, is that we design each event with the adult participant in mind. Since there is a variety of learning styles, so too our events use a variety of methods to achieve learning objectives. For example, in our Giving and Receiving Feedback workshops, we use written texts, validated data, and lecture for those internal learners who prefer to read and listen. We use small group discussion and role plays for the external learners who prefer to discuss and apply, and we use back on the job work aids for mature learners, who need a way to relearn or sometimes remember the skills after a period of time has passed. We try to employ a lot of different methods in order to meet the wide variety of needs of our participants.

Wright

You mentioned that your workshops have helped leaders increase their effectiveness with your models. Can you share an example of a typical ah-hah moment?

Duval

Sure. If you'd indulge me, I'd like to give you two. The first is a story I often tell about a young new manager. It's typical in that it involves a regular guy trying to do his job the best way he can. As I stated earlier, one of our workshops uses a model for giving and receiving feedback. When the TLD instructor asked the managers how many performance appraisals they had to do, this gentleman said, sounding a little intimidated, "17." The instructor asked him what his biggest fear was about the whole process, and he said, "The entire process." The workshop is a two-parter. Participants have a small back-at-work assignment to do during the month between each session. In this case, this manager completed all 17 performance appraisals as his own personal back-at-work assignment. When asked about the advantages to using the model, he remarked that he was able to get his employees to reveal aspects of themselves he never thought possible, and he was able to connect with them in order to set individual action plans for performance development. He actually said that he enjoyed the process so much that they were going to use it informally on a quarterly basis and in those instances, his team was going to give him feedback as well. Clearly, this one thing changed this man's leadership style. Another ah-hah moment is a little more personal. Like many other people, I too am challenged by the implications of my leadership philosophy. I had been working with the Knoxville Museum of Art Strategic Planning Committee to create the museum's mission and vision. When the last session ended, a small group was charged with creating the final product. Well, you know how that goes. As time passed I received no information or status reports, and I just naturally assumed they had dropped the ball. Recently, the director asked me out to lunch, and during lunch, he commented how productive and empowering the whole process was. And how it had been so successful for him and seemed to re-energize both the board and the museum staff. I was a little puzzled. It was when he continued to talk about their dynamic new vision statement that I had my own ah-hah moment. Sitting before me was an empowered leader. Now was the time for me to step aside. He no longer needed me to guide and lead him in the right direction. He was on the right path of his own choosing. I think that as your leadership influence reaches people, you get to see how it goes through them and on to others. Therefore, I've begun to build my business by surrounding myself with highly capable leaders who make things happen, and as a result, TLD will be better and stronger for it.

Wright

Which leaders in your life served as examples and mentors?

Duval

In addition to Mr. Mitchellson, another early mentor of mine was the owner of a restaurant who really knew how to motivate his employees as well as achieve his business objectives. In the restaurant business often you find people feel as if their lives aren't their own because they are at the mercy of their work schedule. For instance, it is difficult to make plans for a vacation because your schedule always changes. To address this Jay Dumont and the rest of his management team would get together three times a year and the employees were allowed to submit their dream schedules. At that meeting, managers would evaluate each employee based on three things—attendance, guest check average, and teamwork. This strategy created an environment that encouraged participation instead of competition. Status points were gained by making each other look good, not bad. And all the while, our guest check averages rose steadily bringing in more revenue to the restaurant. Other benefits that I now see included low turnover, because once you got your dream schedule, you were more likely to want to keep it. Since the meetings were conducted three times a year, not only was there motivation to stay at the top, people didn't want to leave and go somewhere else. What's more, it attracted the best people in the business. Jay's strategy was to have the best people, the best food, and the most inviting atmosphere, and he did it by creating an environment where the staff enjoyed their jobs. To me that's crucial leadership. When people enjoy their jobs, things get done. So, my take-away from that experience, David, was the power of teamwork opposed to the dysfunction that occurs when group objectives are based solely on individual achievement. Of course, I've had other wonderful role models. I've also learned something from the leaders and participants in our workshops. Each session I am amazed at the power and potential I see unleashed in people day in and day out.

Wright

Are there any other leadership core competencies to consider in today's business environment?

Duval

I truly believe it helps to be a whole-brain thinker. By this, I mean leaders must have the flexibility to use whichever part of the brain is required for any given situation. When reviewing financial information, one needs to think analytically. When a leader is required to attend to the needs of others, he or she needs to use empathy and emotion. Leaders should enjoy diversity and capitalize on the variety that is around them. Leaders should be honest about their own improvement opportunities and surround themselves with teams of people with complimentary attributes. In addition, I believe strongly that leaders should continue to establish challenging goals and objectives, and they should communicate their expectations often and consistently throughout the team and organization. It shouldn't just be a once-a-year thing. It should be the mantra that guides the staff throughout the year.

Wright

Speaking of change in business environment, how does your company adjust its "Workshops That Work" to the various types and sizes of organizations?

Duval

One of the advantages of being in the business of improving team and individual performance is that these issues affect a wide variety of organizations, both large and small. We can reach into our bag of tools and tricks in order to provide just the right mix of services. Some clients prefer that TLD develop and deliver the workshops, like ALSTOM Power, Square D, and Nashville Electric Service. However, other clients like Saturn Motors Corporation, for example, prefer that we develop the workshops and have their internal resources facilitate the sessions themselves.

Wright

Finally, Toni, what important questions do today's leaders have to answer?

Duval

First and foremost, I think leaders should start each day asking the questions, "How can I be of service to my team and to my company? And, "What impact can I have today?" These questions place the focus on others instead of ourselves, and this other centric thinking, when combined with strategic planning and excellent communication and influence skills, is a formula for success.

Wright

Well, I think you have given me a lot to think about in our *Conversation on Leadership*. I do appreciate all this time that you've taken with me this morning. I really do think you're on the right track.

Duval

Thank you, David, it was my pleasure talking with you today.

Wright

Today we have been talking to Toni Duval. She is founder and president of TLD-Training and Leadership Development, which was established in 1994. She has over 22 years of experience in the industry, and her passion and energy, as we have found out today, underlie the value of all the programs that she delivers to all of her clients. Thank you so much, Toni.

Duval

Thank you, David.

About The Author

Toni Duval is founder and president of TLD—Training and Leadership Development. She has been in the training and development field for over twenty years, and her clients include many from the Fortune 500 list as well as mid-sized and large businesses in a wide variety of industries. Ms. Duval has traveled extensively throughout North America putting her passion and energy into her TLD learning events, which include leadership and team skills workshops, retreats, and customized learning activities.

Toni L. Duval

TLD-Training and Leadership Development

Phone: 865.588.4290

www.tldconsultants.com

Chapter 14

JAMES T. TURNER, PH.D.

THE INTERVIEW

David E. Wright (Wright)

Today we are talking with Dr. James T. Turner, Ph.D. Dr. Turner knows leadership, as he has focused his career on developing and analyzing leadership characteristics from a logical perspective. He has also held a variety of leadership roles in government and business. He understands first hand the difficult decisions leaders must make, whether in the battlefield or the board room. He is a prolific author, and he has written or edited eight books and numerous articles. He has appeared on television shows such as ABC's *Nightline*, PBS's *Market Watch*, CBS's *Things Considered*, and over 150 radio programs. He has been featured in national consumer publications, *Fortune* magazine, *Glamour*, *Modern Healthcare*, *Entrepreneur* magazine and *The Wall Street Journal*. Currently Dr. Turner is president of International Assessment Services, Inc., a threat management company, as well as being a consultant for Leadership Consulting, VHA, a healthcare alliance. He has worked with a wide range of companies including Compaq, Hewlett Packard, VHA Leadership Conference, American Airlines, California State Automobile Association, Federal Credit Unions Association, Controller of the Treasury, U.S Forestry Service, ASIS, BellSouth, Lockheed Martin,

San Francisco General Medical Center, VHA Nursing Leadership, Dartmouth Hitchcock Medical Center, Hamot Medical Center and Kaiser Permanente. Dr. James Turner, welcome to *Conversations on Leadership*.

James T. Turner (Turner)

David, I'm really glad to be here today.

Wright

What is the driving force behind DeltaForce Leadership?

Turner

Well David, I took the concepts that I learned over years, working in industry and business, and said, "There's got to be a better way to do this." The impact we have seen on employees and companies from really poor leadership is devastating, and the price that people pay is enormous for not having built cadres of great leaders in their organizations. Delta Force Leadership establishes the commitment to the highest quality, the greatest innovation, and the most flexibility for companies as a driving force.

Wright

How did it all get started?

Turner

Well, it got started in a funny sort of way. I got brought in by the Army; I was one of those people who had the opportunity to serve their country. I had a nice job. I was doing a job in Savannah, Georgia. We had a new baby, and getting settled in. Then one day this guy, Col. Charlie Beckwith, came knocking at my door, and I opened the door, and here is this huge bear of a man. He filled the doorway. He said, "I need you." I said, "For what?" He said, "You don't need to know for what; I just need you. Your country needs you." And from there he upset my life dramatically. He did promise me one thing, "I'll take you places you never dreamed; I'll show you things you never expected to see." And he kept his promise.

Wright

I see something called, "Undercover Buzz." What's that all about?

Turner

"Undercover buzz" is something important for entrepreneurs, small companies, large companies, whether you are a manager in a little company or a manager in a Fortune 500. It's incredibly important to be able to create this concept of an undercover buzz. People are going to talk about you; so you might as well be able to control, focus, and direct how they talk about you. You want to be able to create this buzz about who's hot, who's not, what's going, what's not, what are the kind of things that are happening. To do this, you need to take a couple of steps. The first thing you have to do as a leader is to create memorable events. People have short memories. We think the way we are today is the way we were three weeks ago, or the way we were six months ago. You can spend huge amounts of time making change, but unless you create some kind of memory marker that says where we've been, where we are going, and where we are now, you'll lose that perspective for your people. A lot of CEOs have different ways of doing this. Employee recognition dinners ought to be the most exciting thing that leaders do. It shouldn't be, "Oh, I don't want to go; I've been to 15 of these things…" It should be the most exciting thing that happens to your employees all year long. The reason these events don't work is because nobody is excited, leaders dread it, it's just another thing they have to do, and they just go through the motions. They don't create a memorable event. And I'll tell you, it means more to people than the money does. One employee told me that the most memorable thing that ever happened to him in his 30-year career was one day, when a new leader had taken over their department, he was in a meeting and the leader asked him to stand up and said, "John, I want to read a letter to you that came from a customer." And he read this letter about the outstanding customer service that John had given the customer, how he had solved the problem and created even greater customer loyalty. John said that meant more to him, when his boss had taken the time to read it in front of his peers, than all the plaques, and all the raises he had ever gotten in his whole 30 years with the company. So you want to create these memorable events.

Second, leaders need to know to share the credit. They need to share it so well they don't take any for themselves. They give it to people on the front line who do the work. It's paradoxical; the more leaders do that, the more credit they get. The more you give away, the more you'll get. Nobody really cares about the awards you get from the magazines of the world. The bottom line is performance, so when you get this credit, you want to give it all away to the people on the front lines.

The next thing is you want to start rumors. I wish I could tell you that you aren't going to have them, but you are, so you might as well start them yourself. In public, talk about all the good things your people are doing, let yourself be overheard. Let people overhear all the cool things that are going on. They will repeat those stories. They just can't keep from repeating rumors. You might as well give good rumors instead of poor rumors. You'll be amazed how many leaders are insensitive to this issue. If you're in a restaurant, you talk about the good stuff, you don't talk about the bad problems. There are ears everywhere. The last point is you have to learn how to ask the right questions so you can teach people to ask you the right questions. There's this big assumption that people know what we do or understand what we do, that they know how to ask us about what we do. The truth is they don't. So, by planning those questions, modeling those questions for your employers, your customers, your interviewers, or anybody else who comes along, you create this great undercover buzz. Before you know it, people are going to be talking about you, your company, your organization. Pretty soon your employees are going to hear this buzz about what a great company it is. They actually swell up; they stand up a little straighter. So, it's a critical element in leadership, but it's something nobody ever talks about.

Wright

I wish I had talked to you 30 years ago. I learned most of these things by happenstance. I had a real estate company that was the number one company in the whole region, the state, and I had wanted to do something memorable. I had been doing those dull things that you just described. So, at the end of the year around Christmas time I would rent an auditorium and invite about a thousand people. It was a real estate business. I would invite everyone that worked for us and everyone we had sold to that year.

Turner

Alright!

Wright

I would spend about $15,000. That was 30 years ago. And I would just make a great big production out of it. I hired a photographer to take pictures of the spouses and all. I get calls sometimes from people who say, "My husband just died and we used that picture on the casket."

Turner

At the funeral, right. And what's $15,000 compared to tripling or quadrupling your sales?

Wright

I went from $22 million to $40 million the next year.

Turner

Wouldn't you like all your investments to pay off like that? Great leaders sometimes stumble on to these things and don't know what they have.

Wright

Here's another thing called "Tradecraft: An uncovering of covered secrets." How does that impact leaders?

Turner

Another strategy I bring out in Delta Force Leadership: Spec Ops Tactics for Winning on the Business Battlefield that most people don't talk about is that every company has secrets. The best secrets you have are those that your competitors don't know that you have. As soon as they know you have a secret, then somebody's trying to get it. You have to teach people how to keep secrets, how to hide secrets. You can actually use the "undercover buzz" to divert attention away from secrets you don't want discovered. You have to teach your people that there are people looking to find information about your corporation. Some secrets are available on the Internet, and if you dig deep enough, you can find them. But, about 20 percent of secrets aren't readily available, so you have to teach your employees how to keep the secrets covered. Hospitals have even gone so far as to post signs in the elevators that say, "Remember: patient information is confidential." When the doors close, the first thing you see is this little plaque reminding you to be careful of what you talk about in the elevator. The reality is we haven't always done that very well. Next, we don't always know what our secrets are. In my work, I ask leaders to sit down and make a list of the most important company secrets. It shouldn't be a list of 500. It should only be a short list. Then, I ask

"How are you protecting these secrets? How do you prevent people from knowing that they exist? If they get too close, how do you divert them away? What are you doing to find out the other guy's secrets? What kind of covert operations do you have? Are you reading their annual reports or government filings? Do you go have dinner at the places where they and their employees have dinner and listen carefully to what people are saying?" It's amazing. I take people up into hotels where they have lounges on the executive floors and I say, "Let's just sit here with a notepad and listen." You would be amazed at the company secrets I learn. I sometimes write them up and send them back to the company with a note that says, "I think you should keep your company's secrets, secret, and be uncovering other people's secrets, not your own."

Wright

That's a good way to get a consultation contract.

Turner

They will call you up and say, "How did you get this?" and "Where did this come from?" And I say, "That's not important. What is important is how many other secrets you may be leaking." It's a good way to get people to focus on those few things that need attention, that you need to hold on to. The government will classify something as secret. I'll read it and wonder why anyone would even care whether you knew this. The thing to do is concentrate on those incredibly few things that are important to the survival of your company, that are important to the strategic plan of your company. And there's another step. Secrets grow old with time. You want to pick your timing for releasing your secrets, for uncovering those things that are covered. They serve as a wonderful tool to divert your competitors, those who are interested in knowing what you are planning to do next. So, tradecraft really means how does one keep secrets, how does one gain other people's information, that is useful in a competitive environment, so you know what you need to know to make the plans that you need. And there's a bunch of technologies about how to do that, how to collect it, how to analyze it, and how to act on it. Great intelligence without any action is worthless.

Wright

I knew I would learn something today. I have decided, just by your last few comments, if I want to promote something for my company,

I'm going to write the press release as though it is a secret that has been uncovered.

Turner

Absolutely. Let someone leak it for you. That way your employees leak it for you, three hours ahead of time. You want to build relationships with the media so that you become a background source. They will come to you for information, and you'll discover things that you didn't even know were happening.

Wright

How can small or medium businesses or entrepreneurs use the spec ops secrets to enhance their outcomes?

Turner

Those nine tactics that come from spec ops that apply to businesses in the leadership arena are vital to any organization, but particularly, to the small or medium business as well as the entrepreneur, because they usually don't have the room for error that big companies do, with a lot of resources and employees. Smaller companies, and entrepreneurs, have a razor thin margin and it's the difference between success and failure. Learning these secrets, learning how to create an undercover buzz if you're a little company, how to get known? And what you want to be known for? How do you create that kind of buzz? How do you make sure, in a little company, that we're all focused in the same direction? It's incredibly important to get that unity of effort that we talk about over and over again, yet we seldom see. One of the characteristics of special ops teams is that every person on that team has an exquisite understanding of the intent of the mission. We make plans and we put detailed operations together, but once you get into the fray, plans have to be adaptive. Companies have to be flexible, teams need to be able to make decisions so that you fulfill the intent you started. The plan may have to change dramatically.

Leadership skills are not natural for most entrepreneurs. Entrepreneurs are creators of products and systems. They are more creators than leaders, and unless they develop leadership skills, they will often destroy their dreams rather than take people places they never dreamed they would go. Special ops tactics will give entrepreneurs that edge. How do you wage psychological warfare? How do you hold on when the dream seems far away? How do you get the people to stay with you? There will always be ups and downs. Venture capital comes and goes. The pressures of outside people, the competitiveness, and the cutting edge. All these issues wear away at your people. This critical variable of waging psychological warfare keeps your people's spirit intact. Courage is incredibly important for entrepreneurs and small business people. You are battling for the hearts of your people because fear creeps in. Is this going to work? Are we really going to be here tomorrow? Do we have enough cash to get through two more days? In big corporations, fear is usually about the internal politics of that company rather than the survival of the company.

Wright

I'm glad you used the word courage, which some people would have defined as "stick-to-itiveness." Stick-to-itiveness is a discipline; courage is character.

Turner

Right. What is the character of the people you need and do they have the discipline to implement? A lot of people get the two confused. You wisely sorted it out. There's character, and then there's the discipline to implement that character. Some people have character but they don't know how to implement it and share it with other people. On the other hand, there are those who have all the techniques in the world, but they have no character.

Wright

Leaders face many challenges. What do you think is the least understood?

Turner

The least understood are how to motivate, direct, fight for their people and how to build real teams while staying alive. Leaders underestimate the challenge it takes to hold a group of people together and accomplish the dream. You know, if I just have a good enough product, isn't that enough? Or if I have good people, isn't that enough? Some companies have wonderful people but no products. Look at the steel industry. Good people worked the front lines but no innovation occurred. Before we knew it, the rest of the world took over and the industry went away. The big challenge today is the auto industry. We have millions of units representing excess capacity in car building capability. It will take incredible leadership at every level, at the union level, at the company level, and at the front line worker level to get through this and maintain America's primary role in that industry or it too, like America's steel mills, can slip away. This is going to be an incredibly difficult decade. I'm not being pessimistic, I think it can be great, but everything we know in business is going to be challenged because of the globalization of the economy and the globalization of the white collar workforce. When it was always blue collar, "it's just manufacturing," we can survive that. The technical skills in which we have been so strong are at risk, the rest of the world is catching up. We've done a wonderful job of educating them, and now, those jobs are going to India, to Ireland, to China, and what is America's place going to be? What are we going to produce to keep us our economy in the forefront of the world; we can't just hold on to what we have. We have to move into the future. It's going to be leaders who motivate, direct, to get this incredible flexibility and incredible focus out of their workforce that will define the success or failure of the American economy.

Wright

In your book, "Threat Assessment: A Risk Management Approach," you talk about risk not only in terms of leadership but as issues needing to be managed. How does threat management apply in increasing performance and improving outcomes?

Turner

Threat assessment serves as a model that can be used over and over again in a company in different kinds of areas. This particular book focuses on human threats, the kind of threats that people create, both inside and outside the corporation. How do you develop a model for understanding that there are all these forces out there, potential hurricanes on the horizon? How do you stay continually prepared for them? The best time for preparing is when things are wonderful. The worst time to buy plywood is three days before the hurricane comes. When I lived on the East Coast, in Savannah, where they had these potential storms fairly regularly, we had the plywood cut, bought, and stored in our garage a year before we needed it. You have to manage these events. They are frightening to people. They can divert energy away from activities that will create profit and value. They can divert people away from accomplishing the objectives you'd like for them to have. We have to handle multiple sets of data rapidly, and it's an ongoing challenge for all of us. It doesn't matter if it's a human threat or a technology threat. Companies have to develop a methodology to sort through the data, to prioritize it. Threat assessment is about building a way of doing that. You have to understand what has the potential to undermine your leadership and your company. One of the key things a leader has to do is root out deception and dishonesty. If the leader is corrupt, that corruption is going to contaminate the whole organization. We've seen that several times in the last few years. A special ops leader cannot tolerate people who distort the data, because it will get people killed. Delta Force Leaders deal with leaders, managers, supervisors, V.P.s, that distort information for their own personal advantage or because they think it will lever them to get promoted. Your Delta Design must communicate that at every level, dishonesty will not be tolerated. This requires a huge degree of personal integrity because people are watching the little things leaders do.

Wright

How do special ops teams make a difference? Don't companies have enough teams?

Turner

When I work with businesses and organizations, I find that they don't have any teams at all. They have bureaucracies, task forces, and conglomerates of people that meet together and produce very little in outcomes. Entrepreneurs sometimes don't understand that they have to build a team around themselves. They have to build a legal team, an accounting team, a marketing team, even if these people don't work for them. Leaders need teams that are loyal to them, who understand their product, and who will succeed or fail with the leader. One of the primary characteristics of a team is that everybody on that team succeeds or fails together. We don't like that. If you look at Americans, all the way through high school, college, professional schools, we are trained as rabid individualists. "I'll succeed over your dead body if I have to." All of us had that one team project that we had to do and we hated it. There's always someone on the team that doesn't pull their weight. We had to get all these people to agree on how we were going to do this project. But that's exactly the set of skills that you need in the real world. Schools don't train people to have those skills. Our culture trains them to work as individuals for their own reward and their own gain. Leaders have to work hard at molding a team together and holding that team accountable. Success comes to the team as a team; failure comes to the team as a team. Think about it. I'll get in trouble with this from my HR friends, but look how we reward people. Why in the world, if we are trying to build a team, do we reward people with individual raises? Either we all get a raise or nobody gets a raise. We engage in these performance practices that actually make it more difficult to get people to work together as a team.

Wright

I remember going to a United Way dinner last week and Dave Gordon, one of the past presidents of NSA was kidding, and he said when he first started speaking, the butterflies were flying in his stomach, and he said they aren't gone, he had just trained them to fly in formation. What you said made me consider something I haven't before; I have more vendors than employees. I need to figure out how to get them on my team.

Turner

That's right. Their success or failure is tied to your success or failure. They can create an undercover buzz for you. They can help you figure out which secrets are worth keeping and which ones are worth letting go. Entrepreneurs and small businesses often live or die based on teams of vendors. I have a team that works around me. I have Liz, who's the branding and marketing guru; I have Russell, the financial accounting guy who keeps me out of trouble; I have Julian, a can-do attorney; I have Sarah, my trusted advisor who will tell me whether something is good or not; I have Michael, my agent who has a great sense of what will and will not work. And all of these people make more money, if I make more money. If I make less; they make less money. So, every serious leader needs to look around and ask whom do I need on my team and then how do we make them a real team member. You can't assume that they know what it is you're doing and where you want to go. You have to communicate that intent to them, clearly, and create a dream into which they can step. Then you've got to get them on board, and tie them to your success or failure.

Wright

With the number of projects that you have ongoing, why you choose to put time into this area called leadership?

Turner

We always talk about the power of one. This is the situation where one person can make a huge difference in the lives of other people for the better or worse. To me, it's not a job, it's a gift to other people. It's a way of giving back to our economy, our culture, and the people with whom we work, that transcends the way other people give back. We've seen the power of one individual for bad. Let's talk about Enron. You have thousands of people who lost faith in the economy. We've seen other leaders like Needleman at Jet Blue, who, when other people were saying, "I see the lines, we have to close, I can't do this," he was saying, "I see an opportunity; we can build something here." If you want to be influential in this culture, you can either be an entertainer, or you can be a leader. A leader can influence the people in your church, the kids on your street, people you work with, the volunteer group, the business group. Leadership is the biggest leverage point in most organizations.

Wright

Finally, you dedicate time to developing leadership in health care. Why this special focus?

Turner

Health care has always been a special passion. My mom was an R.N. for 40-plus years and worked to improve that system. One thing she asked me to do when she was very elderly, and failing in health, she said, "Please spend some of your time trying to make this thing work, because health care is a microcosm of American life." It's the one place everybody meets. And it pulls together all the diverse elements in American culture. Technology. People. Leadership. Money. Life or death decisions, they all come together in this one place. Health care has taken the leftovers of everybody else. In health care, we have been terribly abusive to leaders. It's like going to the swimming pool where you see the parent throw the kid in, saying, "Kid, you're going to learn how to swim." And then he says, "If he doesn't come up for the third time, I'll go get him/her." The kid may learn to swim, but they don't like water very much. There's a real trust issue there from now on. Then you see the other parent, who takes the time to ease the kid into the water, and the parent mentors, coaches, guides, directs, models the skill, and builds independence. The kid then loves the water. In health care, we have tended to be the first parent rather than the latter. We have thrown these technical people into these roles, watched them sink, and then talked about how bad they are. Health care is a commodity that every one of us will use, sooner or later. So, it's important to all of us that we help these people succeed. Thirty to forty percent of all nurses who leave, if you ask them later why they left, it's not the money, it's not the working conditions, although that can be really tough, it's the quality of their leaders. We are never going to solve the nursing shortage other health care labor shortages, until we deal with developing quality leaders. Leaders able to mentor, lead, guide and direct, not just throw them in the water and let them sink.

Wright

I want you to know I appreciate your taking all this time to be with us today. It's obvious you know what you're talking about.

Turner

Thank you for having me.

Wright

Today we've been talking with Dr. James T. Turner, who indeed knows leadership. He has worked in health care and in business and he understands first hand all the difficult decisions that leaders must make. Thank you so much for being with us on *Conversations on Leadership*.

About The Author

James T. Turner, Ph.D., knows leadership. Not only has he focused his career on developing and analyzing leadership, he has also held leadership roles in government, health care, and business. He understands the difficult decisions leaders must make. A prolific author and speaker, Dr. Turner has written/edited five books and numerous articles including, *Threat Assessment: A Risk Management Approach* [Haworth, 2003] and *Delta Force Leadership: Special Ops Tactics to Win on the Business Battlefield* [2004].

James T. Turner, Ph.D.
Delta Force Leadership, #141
10755 Scripps Poway Parkway
San Diego, California 92131
Phone: 760.789.9484
Fax: 760.789.9453
Email: jturner@deltaforceleadership.com

Chapter 15

PAUL H. BATZ

THE INTERVIEW

David E. Wright (Wright)

On his 40th birthday, Paul Batz was elected Chairman of the Board for one of America's most influential non-profit, social service organizations—Lutheran Social Service of Minnesota. Batz is a fiery personality and an engaging young leader. By day he is an executive coach, and a driving force at MDA Consulting Group, one of the fastest growing leadership consulting firms in the country. The firm helps leaders build higher performing organizations through talent management, leadership development and change consulting. Paul Batz is an expert in business development, executive credibility and building the thrill of accountability. He has earned the reputation as a dynamic professional speaker and a courageous coach who challenges executives to grow as leaders. His first book, *Inspire, Persuade, Lead: Communication Secrets of Excellent Leaders,* is in its second printing. Paul Batz, welcome to *Conversations on Leadership.*

Wright

Paul, I can't imagine someone waking up in the morning in junior high school and deciding to become an executive coach. How did that happen for you?

Paul H. Batz (Batz)

You're right. It didn't happen overnight. Becoming an executive coach has been a natural progression of the experiences I've had during my career. Looking back—as far back as high school and college—there has been a series of entrepreneurial adventures that set the stage for me to get into coaching. When I was young, I had the opportunity to meet a lot of successful, powerful people. I realized they had common two traits: their minds worked really fast and they liked to be challenged. I could relate. I've been blessed—or you could say cursed—with a really quick mind. I also have an innate sense to call it straight and the instincts to ask the tough questions—all of which are important skills for an executive coach. And, I've had a lot of opportunity to hone these skills.

Most of my professional experience has been in the advertising and public relations industry. My favorite role was as a business development and strategy consultant. In that role, you meet a lot of talented, senior executives, and you get the privilege of asking some very pointed questions. Questions like: What do you want to be known for? Why would anyone feel compelled to choose your offering over any of your competitors? What is the driving concept of your success, and can you sustain it? I observed that more often than not, powerful executives stumbled over the answers to these questions, and I often found myself "coaching" these individuals on how to take complex issues and articulate them in ways that would get others motivated and willing to do what the executive needed. So, while I still thought of myself as a PR consultant, I was really doing executive coaching.

In hindsight, my experience in advertising and public relations was incredibly important because the foundation of that industry is communication—message development, articulation, clarity. As an executive coach, I challenge clients to come to grips with what the people in their organization expect from them as leaders. One of the simplest exercises is helping a leader understand "clarity." People crave clarity around their goals, roles and priorities. Business today is complicated; the role of the executive is complex. It's a powerful thing to remind them of what their people need from them, and what it feels like to be well led.

Wright

Well led...hmm. That's an interesting perspective. What do you think is behind feeling well led?

Batz

That's a great question. In general, when people are well informed, they feel well led. When I wrote my first book, it was about the role leaders have as influencers and how they use communication as a leadership strategy. During the process of writing that book, I developed the subject matter by asking people, "Hey, do you have a favorite leader? What does it mean to you when you say someone is your favorite leader? What does that person do specifically?" The stories I heard gave me good insight into some pretty fascinating concepts about "favorite leaders." Common themes that I heard included: "They [leaders] go out of their way to make people feel good about themselves. They communicate with clarity. They are engaging in how they go about introducing change and how they go about capturing the hearts and minds of people who are important to their success." The bottom line is that the people who feel well led are well informed. They understand what the strategic priorities are in the organization. They understand their value and their role in the organization. The best leaders really are the best communicators.

Wright

You're right, it does sound simple when you put it that way. But, let's back up for minute. The concept of "engaging leader" sounds a little soft to me. With the business climate of this decade, isn't it reasonable to think that the most successful leaders need a little more bottom line orientation?

Batz

That's a good point. I think engaging leaders actually do need a very keen bottom line orientation—don't let the term fool you. A couple of my favorite leaders—Dick Kovacevich at Wells Fargo and Mark Zesbaugh at Allianz Life—are both examples of engaging leaders with a bottom line orientation. But, they know how to use communication and influence to motivate others, they thrive on accountability and have cultivated an appreciation for executing a business plan that is thrilling instead of scary. Employees describe Kovacevich and Zesbaugh as engaging leaders. That takes real leadership and talent.

Wright

Doesn't the concept of accountability usually dig up fear and concern? I believe many of the experts talk about how important it is to drive out fear in the organization. What's the secret to building the thrill of accountability into an organization without driving fear into people?

Batz

At MDA Consulting Group, we believe that leadership is about creating clarity and commitment in an organization. That takes real hard work. We feel that accountability—accomplishing the things that you promised you would accomplish—can best be done by hooking both the hearts and minds of people. It means leaders have to work at both the emotional level and the intellectual level when they want to create true commitment around goals and objectives. To help people understand this, we work with the concept of the three C's: clarity, commitment and consequences. It works with leaders at all levels. When leaders concentrate on hooking the hearts and minds of people around clear goals and objectives, accompanied by clear positive and negative consequences...it changes how they think about leadership. It's interesting to get their reactions to having their very first accountability conversation with the three C's in mind. Many realize that they haven't really taken the time to think through exactly what success will be. They haven't articulated with real clarity what a job well done looks like when they reach the end. Often times, they are exceptionally general and vague, and nobody is watching closely enough to see whether anything really gets done. And, of course, if no one really knows what success looks like, it's difficult to question whether it's been achieved. Defining success is important because real leaders celebrate specific accomplishments.

Wright

This all sounds really great and kind of simple—in a consulting sort of way! But how does it really work?

Batz

Well, it starts with the leader. The leader has to be in a situation where they actually feel like they're holding themselves accountable for something. So, that the organization can see, literally, that they're holding themselves accountable and that the organization is better off because of it. It's about making a choice that says "I'm going to be the one who sets the pace for the organization." After that, I really think the fuel that fires the thrill of accountability is well-placed praise. People need praise to get the accountability concept burning in an organization. The best leaders routinely catch people doing things right. They catch them doing things right far more often than they find them doing things wrong. You know, when I talked about being well led before? You can ask any employee whether or not they feel appreciated and they'll say, "Yes," if they know their leaders are in tune with what's going on and if they feel their good work is being appreciated. Most of the time when leaders hold performance conversations they start with "I'm concerned about this thing or that issue." That's not very motivating. And, it's not about being able to take criticism or being willing to change some behaviors. It's just easier to give your heart and mind if you know that deep down the leader really appreciates what you're doing. That's the bottom line around influencing people. When you start catching your team doing things right, when you start talking to individuals about the things they are doing right it sets the flywheel in motion. It's the small wins that show people you care and the new way of operating is winning out over the old.

There is one other thing about this that needs to be said—most of the really good leaders I know are really good storytellers. They have captured lots of the small wins that happened in their organization in short, crisp stories. These short—sometimes 30 second-stories say, "Hey, we are on the right track. We are doing things right." People remember those stories and they go out and replicate that behavior. It's a powerful leadership technique.

Wright

Will you give our readers an example? Perhaps you have a story about how this worked for a successful leader?

Batz

Yeah, that's a good idea. Let me tell you a story about a terrific COO and General Manager at a large division of a multi-billion dollar national organization. We'll call him Bill. Bill is a new leader in an organization that has been very successful during the past 25 years. The organization has grown, primarily with a very entrepreneurial attitude. It's a national company that has entrepreneurs on the ground in local markets all over the continental United States. They have built their reputation one market at a time. The formula that they used to get to this level of success was simple. It was a standardized product line delivered with flexible, customized local-market savvy. The entrepreneurs really performed as—I use the phrase affectionately—"the Marlboro Man." They were out doing their own thing and they were really proud of it. But, like many businesses, they recognized that their market was changing. Different demographic buying patterns, access to new information and new choices resulted in a consumer base that had less urgency to buy this company's product. Bill's challenge was to convince this organization that the business proposition needed to be exactly opposite if they were actually going to succeed long term. They needed much more customized products—products that the consumer could actually design themselves, but with a much more standardized method of delivery. Needless to say, this was a shock to the culture and the organizational systems because they had been glorifying the people who did things their own way and there were very few standardized processes across the whole company. One of the first things Bill had to do was convince people he wasn't out to do this for his own good. He needed to actually show people that he lived the mission and the passion for the organization and that he was in tune with what was actually going on. He needed to demonstrate his own commitment. Then, before he asked people to change, he had to think a lot deeper about what, exactly, he was looking for. That's the clarity part we talked about. Previously, the leaders had never articulated success in any other way than just the numbers they expected at the end of the year. Bill had to think through some of the small steps necessary to make the changes he expected. It wasn't easy or fun, and he didn't succeed right away. The organization rejected the idea of the negative consequences for not going along with Bill's ideas. The positive consequences were mostly based on the "Marlboro Man" concept— they could do what they wanted, when they wanted, and they were incented by a compensation structure that supported doing business the old way. Things got ugly when Bill laid out the negative consequences that would come with not being accountable to the new plan. But, he didn't dwell on the problems. Instead, he got his senior team involved in the field sales activity. He sent them out into the marketplace to look for things that were going right. Then he increased the frequency of his communications, and he started sharing the stories his senior team collected. He started sharing more real, live data from specific parts of the business that were doing things differently and growing. Slowly, he started to see better growth and better profits return. He started to see more engaged employees. He started to see real growth where reps were actually starting to offer customized products instead of standardized ones. All along the way he had to really perform as the chief storyteller. He had to open up new communication channels. They did weekly conference calls where all they did was share success stories. They changed the content of the newsletter. They changed the context of the management team meetings. They changed the context of what was going on in the sales accountability meetings. It was all really around "what's working." I can tell you that they're well on their way. Growth has been impressive and profitability is back to where they expected.

Wright

So, what's the single most important thing leaders need to do in order to start building a high performing culture where accountability is a thrilling rather than scary concept?

Batz

In the case of Bill, the single most important thing was to make sure that he was willing to be held accountable himself. You can't support a double standard. Unfortunately, we see that happening all the time. There are people who are preaching change, change, change, but they reinforce the double standard by not sharing what they are willing to be held accountable for, or really never allow people to examine their own performance. Deep down inside any organization, people want to have clear goals and celebrate in their own special way when they achieve those goals. But, if you're going to be a leader who won't let people know what you're expecting of yourself, then people around you can't share in your own success.

Wright

Let's talk a little bit about your passion for non-profits. Do you believe you can build the thrill of accountability into the quasi-government social service world?

Batz

Absolutely. The concepts are the same. It's a reality that non-profits, especially social service organizations, measure their success differently. But, essentially the practice is the same. With the difficulty of today's funding environment, many non-profits have survival as their overarching goal, and that makes good sense! But it's tricky, because there is a really fine line between celebrating survival as the goal and unintentionally allowing people to settle into small expectations. We believe that all employees, whether in a non-profit or profit organization, want to be part of a dynamic, healthy, growing organization. It doesn't matter if you're in a manufacturing plant or at a social service organization. It's just way more fun when you're growing and serving needs at the same time.

Remember, the thrill of accountability basically is a support system to help people do what they say they're going to do. It's an expectation that comes from the whole of the organization. When a charitable organization that runs on the thinnest of margins allows the organization to run in the red year after year after year, the expectation is clear—losing money means success. The best non-profits that I know are accepting the fact that they have razor-thin margins, but they use those razor-thin margins as a motivator to stay in the black. As leaders start to demonstrate the ability to deliver a margin over and over again, they start to really believe that they can be both healthy as an organization and carry out their mission. That's one of the reasons that I'm so excited about the work I do for LSS of Minnesota. No one will argue that the climate right now for funding social services is the worst we've seen in decades. The number of people in need is increasing dramatically—and these people have very, very basic needs. Our challenge as a leadership core at LSS of Minnesota is to keep ourselves focused on what we expect for success today, and what we expect the organization will be like in the future. When we do start to pull out of this, where is the organization going to be headed? Because if we do our work right today, when that turnaround comes, we'll be set to slingshot to a whole new level. That's inspiring.

Wright

What have you learned from the corporate world that you think you could try and apply in the non-profit world and vice-versa?

Batz

The very best non-profits are driven by a mission, but they also have a very deep sensibility, in a corporate way, for operating as a healthy entity, for having some operating margins, for having very strong processes in place to ensure the organization stays healthy long term and can continue to provide the essential services. The very best corporations that I know have the same corporate sensibilities that we might think of in terms of business processes and operating margins, but they wear their mission on their sleeve. It's a misnomer to say "There is no mission without margin." I think the opposite is true. "There is no margin without mission in the corporate world."

You have to have a group of people who are passionately engaged with some sense of the greater good. The greater good has to be bigger than shareholder value. I can tell you that in working with powerful leaders from an executive coaching standpoint, one of the most powerful things that we can do for them is to really help them connect with their larger sense of mission for their leadership. We're asking questions like, "What is your leadership legacy?" "When you are done with this job, what do you want your organization to have accomplished?" "What do you want people to say about you as their leader?" In many ways, that helps people get really connected with both the idealistic, visionary part of their lives and also the day-to-day operations of what they're going to do as a leader. And, it always helps.

Wright

How were you able to apply this thinking to your own business? I understand that MDA is really growing with a focus on leadership consulting. What's working right about the business?

Batz

We believe that successful leaders really understand the double-edged sword of their jobs. They know that the opportunity for leadership is one of the most invigorating roles in any organization, but it's nowhere as easy as it sounds. They seldom get straightforward feedback, and there are times when it's a lonely, isolated job. Some of the expectations aren't very fair and the challenges can often seem overwhelming. That's one of the reasons why executive coaches exist. We provide a safe place to think out loud. Ultimately our job is to help leaders develop the people and the resources they need in order to improve their organization.

MDA Consulting Group was founded 22 years ago as a psychological consulting firm. The psychological tools and science are powerful in helping people understand themselves and their impact on other people. Today we call ourselves a leadership consulting firm. At our best, the executive teams we work with count on us to push the edge of growth and make sure they have the right change strategies in place so they can be confident in making decisions about the capabilities of their people and, really, the capabilities of their organization. We think it's a terrific thing to do for a living. And lately the fuel for the growth has been concentrating our energy into creating long-term partnerships with leaders. We have learned to think of ourselves as an extra set of eyes and ears bringing an outside perspective from other leaders to help look around corners and support people when they need to be supported. And, frankly, to challenge them with some really tough feedback and advice when they need it. So far, month after month, year after year they keep coming back. That's what makes it exciting.

Wright

What successes are you celebrating?

Batz

The most basic success we're celebrating is our clients' success! We bring the courage and experience necessary to be decisive in leveling with leaders about the changes they need to make to reach their goals. When it works, it's invigorating to celebrate the successes of our clients. And that fills us with a deep sense of purpose—especially in this tough economy. Like many other businesses, we went through some rough times right before and following September 11th . It forced us to bring greater clarity to our services—and it's worked. Internally, our staff is passionate about what we do for a living. I don't know about you, but it's a lot more fun to hang out in an organization where people are engaged and really in love with their work than it is to hang out in an organization that has the opposite going on.

You know, I think we started this conversation by asking how in the world does a person connect with powerful people and become a respected executive coach. I think it all comes from the courage to develop deep relationships with people where you really know their hopes and dreams and you can celebrate their successes along the way with them. Just knowing that you've had a role in their success brings a terrific sense of satisfaction.

Wright

Well, today we've been talking to Paul Batz who is an expert in business development, executive credibility and building the thrill of accountability. He has earned the reputation as a dynamic professional speaker who challenges and inspires executives to grow as people and as leaders. As we have found out today, I think he knows what he is talking about.

Paul, thank you so much for spending this much time with me today in *Conversations on Leadership.*

Batz
You're welcome.

About The Author

Paul Batz is an results-oriented executive coach, author and speaker with MDA Consulting Group—one of the fastest growing leadership consulting firms in America. Paul is an energetic, passionate speaker and inspiring coach who understands how to motivate growth and change in dynamic business environments. His first book *Inspire Persuade Lead* is a teaching tool in corporate and university leadership programs. He frequently counsels clients in the areas of influence, accountability, leadership communication and executive presence.

Paul H. Batz

MDA Consulting Group

150 South Fifth Street, Suite 3300

Minneapolis, Minnesota 55402

Phone: 612.332.8182

Email: pbatz@mdaconsultinggroup.com

www.mdaconsultinggroup.com

Chapter 16

ALAN KEYES

THE INTERVIEW

David E. Wright (Wright)

Alan Keyes' powerful conservative message resonates for millions of Americans from all walks of life and every geographic region, who share his vision of a morally based government founded on the principles embodied in our nation's Declaration of Independence. The Republican Presidential candidate received his Ph.D. in Government Affairs in 1979 from Harvard University. He served in the U.S. Foreign Service and on the staff of the National Security Council by President Ronald Reagan in 1983. He was Assistant Secretary of State for International Organization Affairs from 1985 to 1987. Following his tenure with the State Department, Ambassador Keyes was president of Citizens Against Government Waste, where he founded CAGW's National Taxpayer Action Day. His political activism continues to challenge both liberal Democrats and those within his own party who fails to support the essential principles upon which the U.S. was founded. Over the past ten years, Ambassador Keyes has been featured at different times on a daily, syndicated talk radio program and television series. He is the author of tow critically acclaimed books, Masters of the Dream: The Strength and Betrayal of Black American and Our Character, Our Future: Reclaiming America's Moral Destiny. It is my sincere pleasure to welcome Dr. Alan Keyes to our program. Alan, welcome and thank you for joining us today.

Alan Keyes (Keyes)

I am glad to be here. Thank you.

Wright

I'm interested in exploring two subjects with you today that I believe are intrinsically linked, and in which I believe you are uniquely qualified to offer our readers insight. I'm speaking of freedom and leadership. Before we dive into the subject matter though, would you explain how you became interested in cultural issues related to our Constitution?

Keyes

I have always been interested. As a graduate student, I spent a lot of time studying the foundations of America's system of self government and the ideas that our founders were following when they put together the constitution and the free way of life that we are supposed to enjoy in America. What has struck me most forcefully over the course of both my studies and experience is that there is a moral foundation for our way of life. Without which it cannot be sustained. That moral understanding, the principles that are articulated in the Declaration of Independence, is essential if liberty is to be properly understood, properly applied and preserved. It requires a certain character in the people and a willingness to look back to our moral heritage and understand its deep roots in respect for the authority of God and the idea that he is the source of our rights and justice. I believe that a right understanding of our way of life both in a political and constitutional sense requires that you take seriously the challenge of moral character to a free people.

Wright

For those of us who are not history experts, can you explain why our Constitution is unique compared to those of other countries?

Keyes

Our Constitution was a result of a unique, providential moment in human history. I think that there were insights involved that were a consequence both of the Christian heritage of our founders and their respect for the need to apply disciplined reason to the challenges of government. That combination led them to acknowledge certain basic principles that were contrary to their own class and personal interest. You had folks who were land owners and slave owners and were acknowledging given the fact that all human beings are created equal; and that God intends for that equality to be the foundation of the sense of justice in any regime. As a result, government has to be based upon consent and structural around institutions of representation. These were things that they believed a just acknowledgement of Gods principles required. At the time, it went against what would be considered the selfish interest of many of them. When you see the human heart responding to principles of right thinking and justice in spite of deep inclinations of passionate interest, I think one has to acknowledge that there is at work a divine grace.

Wright

In a broad sense, do you see a correlation between our country's recent interpretation and application of the Constitution and the personal lives of individual citizens of the United States?

Keyes

Sadly, I think so. We have been in a period when our understanding of our constitutional life has become very undisciplined. We are not living according to the principles that are reflected in the Constitution. When a great deal of ignorance is combined with manipulation on the part of the elite's in the society it turns us away from the path that the nation was set by our founders and toward a path that could lead to Tierney. That is dictatorship by the few instead of a government of the people, by the people, and for the people. That approach reflects the licentiousness that has become more and more prevalent in the entertainment culture, in the media and in their personal lives of a lot of folks. We are acting as if there are no standards of behavior, no standards of judgment and responsibility. But, if at the end of the day there is no basis for distinguishing between right and wrong in one's personal life, then how is one going to maintain rights that are drawn from a sense that there is a transcended authority who commands respect for these rights? So, I think there is a definite connection between the erosion of a personal moral sense and the erosion of our understanding of the moral principles that underlie our way of life.

Wright

Political commentators argue about the role of government in our lives. Some are proponents of larger, more "active" government. Others, like you, believe less is better. To what extent do you think government can effect an individual citizen's ability to succeed, to reach their goals and fulfill their dreams?

Keyes

I think the government should operate the way our system of traffic lights and the enforcement of traffic laws operates. When you are driving along the road, nobody is dictating to you where you are going. But you do have to respect the rules that allow everybody to use the road in a way that doesn't lead to accidents that would make it impossible for people to get where they were going. I think that's the right understanding of how a free way of life ought to operate. The government is there to help us create an environment that facilitates the ability of individuals and the associations they form. Government cannot substitute for individual effort, responsibility, organization and preparation and should not attempt to do so. There has developed a combination of a mentality of false compassion, which seeks to use the government for all kinds of welfare purposes in substitution for the initiative and responsibility of the individual. At the same time, that sense of compassion leads to a welfare mentality. It also leads to two things: A sense of entitlement, which then can substitute for a sense of personal responsibility and also a willingness to put up with all kinds of dictation and domination in pursuit of the welfare objective. At the end of the day, you end up sacrificing real freedom. I think that the government can be a facilitator. But when it attempts to substitute government action and power for the initiative, discipline and responsibility of individuals, then you get into a situation in which freedom is undermined. And ultimately, I think the results that are produced will mirror the failures of social estates that we have seen in that last century.

Wright

Along with the seriousness of this county, you made an impressive run for the Presidency a few years ago. Few would argue that you won every debate you entered. What kind of leader would you have been as President of the United States? Will you describe the principles by which you would lead this nation?

Keyes

Well, I think that is pretty simple. I have tried in my public life to do what—if I understand him correctly—Lincoln tried to do, which is to apply the principles and insights that are in our Declaration of Independence to the politics and laws and policies of the United States. So, you begin from the premise of God's existence and his authority, you go to the conclusion of the emphasis on human liberty and responsibility and you formulate policies that seek to promote that liberty to preserve the moral foundations that are necessary for that responsibility. Also, to defend in the world a sense of securing from foes and from domestic deterioration the Constitution that allows us to realize these principles. I think that approach allows one to look at a whole range of subjects—economic subjects, foreign policy subjects, and of course, the issues that involve moral judgments and moral challenge issues of our times. It allows one to look at them in a way that will reflect choices that contribute to preserving this constitutional system and the blessings of liberty that it is supposed to entail.

Wright

The recent scandals in corporate America have reminded many Americans that great leaders must be men and women of character. To what do you attribute this failure in leadership and what solutions would you offer a country hungry for stronger leadership?

Keyes

I think the main problem, whether it is in the private sector economic enterprises, is the sense of selfishness, self interest, unbridled from any over arching sense of discipline or responsibility to the higher authority of God. That leads to a situation in which people do what they can get away with. Instead of approaching every situation in terms of what your responsibilities and obligations might be to your family and to the community; you are thinking about how to maximize your own success. If you need to do that at the expense of others, at the expense of moral decency, that is ok as long as you succeed. The notion that somehow success can substitute for moral principle is in all areas of our life hurting people. It also reflects itself in a personal ethic at the sexual level that seeks to use people for sexual pleasure without regard to pro-creation. The mentality whether you are pursuing money or pleasure is the same at the expense of those decent holds that can only be founded upon respect for moral principles and standards of right and wrong. I think we have seen a lot of that spirit. It is what leads leaders in business to disregard the interest of stockholders and to look for ways around and through the rules and ethical standards, so that they can maximize the bottom line come what may. I think that mentality, the unbridled self-interest, the ramped selfishness, is precisely a problem and is precisely the result of the destruction of an over arching sense of moral standards that then applies in all these different areas of life.

Wright

You know that used to bother me to no end, but now I have a 14-year-old daughter that would argue that she is 15 because her birthday is in thirty days. It is very difficult for me to bring out those principles of character. I keep her in church, but the government is not helping all that much.

Keyes

Well, I think that is one of the difficulties we face. The first and most important thing I have discovered as parent is that you cannot do it alone. By that, I not only mean the partnership between husband and wife and the support needed from family and friends, I basically mean God. I have discovered in the course of being a parent, that the situations you face, break your heart. They face you with a sense of your own limitations and inadequacies. You find yourself time and time again resorting to prayer and down on your knees humbled by the sense that your are not adequate to provide the items that your children need. That leads to your reliance on God. That reliance is perhaps the most important thing we can pass along to our children. Yet, it is challenged everywhere in our society. You are taught to rely on money, government, power, science and so forth. All of these things are pushing themselves forward as a substitute for ones reliance on Gods will and favor and guidance. I think this is one of the saddest consequences of the secularization of our entire way of life. It has resulted and been promoted by people who have a false understand of what our society is about. They have used arguments like the separation of church and state to reach conclusions that end up separating God from every aspect of our society and our culture as well as our politics.

Wright

Many of our readers are leaders in corporate America, small business, local churches and volunteer organizations. Would you take a moment and reflect of the leadership positions you have had through the years and share some practical insights that would empower people to be better leaders?

Keyes

I come from a perspective where almost everything I have done has involved efforts to work with and organize people at the grass roots around issues and purposes of common concern. Whether in the economic or the moral realm. In the arena, the most important thing that I have had to both learn and remember is that I was involved in enterprises that were all exercises in voluntary cooperation. The people were attracted to the things I was doing and were accepting the leadership that I could provide. They had come because their hearts were dedicated to a cause and a purpose that we shared. They were in that sense, not just tools or instruments; they were to be respected as folks who represented the very same principles that I was pursuing and wanted to respect. I think that is at the heart of it, the real meaning of self-government. We are people who are working together on a basis of equality, trying to pool our talents and resources. If one is in a position of leadership, it is not so much domination, as it is an effort to bring out different aspects that are contained within all those abilities and talents. I think that is what achieves the best results. None of us can do anything on our own. Leaders in particular have to remember that leadership is really defined in terms of success, in terms of how well you get others to make that contribution. So, you are not out there acting on your own or imposing your will on your own. What I have found over the years, is that you have to have a strong sense of where you are going and why you think it is important. As well as what the principles are that govern your judgment. You also have to be willing to listen to people, because you wouldn't have them around you if they didn't represent the abilities, talents, insights, and perspectives that are need to achieve the goal. I think it is quite foolish sometimes that way folks will be blinded by their own sense of what need to be done. You need to look through the eyes of others that you are working with, because they may be seeing things that are vital to your success.

Wright

Some of the things I have listened to recently are just beyond my imagination. Such as, the President asking for 87 billion dollars to send to one purpose. Number one, that is a mind boggling number that is hard for me to get my mind around. Second, I'm wondering if I have any choice in that matter at all.

Keyes

I think over all, of course we do. We are making choices. We will again in the year 2004. We will decide who goes to the White House, who goes into Congress and who goes to the Senate. A lot of times, I think people are wasting their votes. They are voting for people they don't think are any good. They take a lesser than evil mentality. If you take the choice of evil what you get is evil. And therefore, don't be surprised when it doesn't work out. I think folks need to start deciding what they think is right, look for people who are standing for those things come what may and casting their vote to reflect their heartfelt beliefs about what is right for the country. A failure to do that is explaining a lot of the mediocrity in the leadership right now. That mediocrity comes at the end of the day because people doubt the courage of their own convictions first; that lack of courage is related to a lack of faith. It is an inability to try to figure out what is your duty and leave the rest to God. I think that lack of a sense that God is watching, that he'll take care of it if you do what is right, the lack of that conviction of faith is leading a lot of people to waste their citizenship and do things that in the end put people in office that shouldn't be there while they go away saying, "Well, I didn't have a choice." In plain fact, most of the time, people do have choices. They just don't have the guts to make those choices that reflect their true convictions.

Wright

You served President Ronald Reagan as Ambassador to the United Nations. What kind of leader do you think Reagan was and can we learn from his successes and failures?

Keyes

I think we definitely can. The thing we have to remember though—that has been forgotten because of the great success of his Presidency—is that Ronald Reagan was a man of principal. For a good part of his career, he was willing to fail for the sake of his principals. He was willing to do things that the people in the political reign said, "No, you can't do that, you have to compromise to get elected, you've got to tone this down so you can get into office." He never did. He was willing to spend twenty years in the political wilderness, working with people of similar conviction and principle. Before, at a juncture critical to this country he was finally elevated to the Presidency. He wouldn't have been the man for the job if he had listened to those people who told him to throw away his principles, to compromise his integrity, to give up the things he believed in for the sake of short term political success. When he got to office the sense that he was somebody who knew who he was, who knew where he stood, who knew in fact what his principles were and who knew that he hadn't come to power for the sake of power was known. He had come to power in order to serve those convictions with respect to limited government, free enterprise, anti-communism, the morals and foundations of society that he had stood for in his public life. It is that sense that he was somebody who came to office with a mission that transcended his own personal ambition or reputation that made him the great President that he was.

Wright

When you consider the party and the people who are in power today, in 2003—I don't want to put you on the spot or talk negatively about any of your friends, I know you are in the republican party— how are they doing do you think? When you consider all the things that you have said about moral character and consciousness of things that is right and wrong. How do you think they are doing generally?

Keyes

I think that in the course of the last several years, we have obviously reached a nadir, in terms of the moral status of political leadership in American life. That nadir was represented, in my personal opinion, by Bill Clinton. I think that we have certainly seen an elevation of standards from that era. In the same time, of course, we have faced a major challenge, which is both a challenge to our security in the form of terrorism and a challenge to our will and resolve, which is a challenge to our moral spirit. I thing the American people have risen to that challenge and they have inspired leaders to come forward and rise to that occasion. We have been able to face this period with a sense of unity and resolve that was reflected in the hearts of the people as they responded to September 11th. A lot of people returned to their understanding that this nation's fate rests ultimately in the hands of God. Therefore, we have to turn to God, ask for his blessings, ask for his guidance and not be ashamed to humble ourselves as a people as we face an era of tremendous danger. Our innocent people are on the front lines of the war that we fight against terrorist who are implementing policies of violence against the inno- cent in order to achieve their objective. I think in that context we have seen folks rise well to the occasion. We have responded to it with forcefulness and resolve and I hope we will continue to do so. So of course, there are other issues which have to do with the underlying integrity of the moral foundations with which we face this crisis. Those issues continue to percolate, sometimes satisfactorily, in terms of leadership, sometimes not. I think we are going to need leaders who are willing to think things through in terms of the principles and requirements of moral leadership in a free society and stand where they need to stand in spite of political calculation. We don't see that all the time and I just keep praying they we will see more of it.

Wright

When you consider all the decisions you have made down through the years, in all aspects of your life, has faith played an important role?

Keyes

I think it has played the decisive role. I can't imagine why I would continue and keep going against the odds except for faith in God and the gratitude that he gives me. That is what I pray for and I have been blessed in that regard. It is the sustaining, underlying premise of my life. I think that has been in found the things that I have been able to do in public life. None of it would have any meaning except I deeply believe that God's will is at work in our human affairs. If we can, to the best of our ability, try to discern what he wishes for us to do. Regardless of how it looks to the world we are on the right path.

Wright

Dr. Keyes, you don't know how much I appreciate you taking all this time with me today to share your views on leadership, success and on the principles of our government. It has been a pleasure visiting with you. Thank you so much for taking the time for this inspiring conversation.

Keyes

Thank you.

About The Author

Alan Keyes, candidate for the 1996 and 2000 Republican Party presidential nominations, founder and chairman of the Board of the Declaration Foundation, and former chairman of the Grace Commission influences the public through a variety of media. He is an author and public speaker on a wide range of national and foreign policy issues; an educator; the writer of a weekly nationally distributed column on current affairs; and the host of *The Alan Keyes Show: America's Wake-up Call*, and a nationally syndicated "call-in" radio talk show. Author of *Our Character, Our Future and Masters of the Dream*, Keyes also served as the U.S. Ambassador to the United Nations Social and Economic Council and as the Assistant Secretary of State for International Organizations.

Alan Keyes

www.AlanKeyes.com

Chapter 17

A. William Bodine, Ph.D.

THE INTERVIEW

David E. Wright (Wright)

We're talking today with William Bodine, chairman of The Investment Advisory Group. Bill's company provides strategic investment and consulting services to major institutions as well as significant private groups, individuals and governments throughout world. His client list includes The World Bank, Goldman Saks, Citicorp, Asian Development Bank, AIG, Indo-Suoz Banque and Mitsubishi.

In addition to being an investment counselor, Bill has served as a CFA Examiner and has been a Supervisory Analyst for the New York Stock Exchange. He has also been an advisor for the Asian Development Bank, DeLoitte Touche and two private equity funds for the Rockefeller Family Office.

He is President of the New York Society of Security Analysts and a Co-Founding Governor of the Association for Investor Management and Research. His titles also include founding director of the International Society of Financial Analysts and director of the Financial Analysts Federation.

Through the course of his work in the world of finance, Bill has spent a lot of time in recent years working in the People's Republic of China. As a result, he has arrived at some intriguing conclusions when it comes to the economic development of that country, particularly how its growth as a superpower is measuring up to our own country's status as a world power. We're looking forward to his sharing some of those insights with us today. Bill, thank you so much for joining us here on *Conversations on Leadership.*

William Bodine (Bodine)
Thank you for having me. It's a pleasure.

Wright
I think that one thing our readers and listeners might be wondering is what qualifies an investment advisor from New York to compare America's status as a superpower to the changing condition of the People's Republic of China.

Bodine
First, my undergraduate education was in political science and economics at UCLA, followed by MBA studies at Harvard Business School and a Ph.D. in finance at Marlborough University in the United Kingdom. These experiences, I believe, have provided me with the disciplines necessary to examine some major issues impacting America and China today.

Second, my professional work has been heavily involved with firms that are serious about research and where my skills have been useful for getting answers, making decisions and, most of all, making money.

Third, I have been lucky enough in my work to have traveled the world extensively for over twenty-five years. In particular, I have spent a fair amount of time in recent years in China, where I have firsthand experience serving as an advisor to Peking University and as chairman of a fund that's investing in China.

Wright
What took you to China in the first place?

Bodine
That all developed about four years ago, when I got involved in the China Mantou fund, a leading mutual fund investing in public equi-

ties in greater China. As I got involved, I had to become familiar with what was going on with government policies and other factors driving China's economic policies. I started making trips over there, and in the process, I had the opportunity to meet government officials and officials at major universities and subsequently was invited to give addresses at major conferences in Beijing and Shanghai. That led to my being a senior advisor at the Peking University Graduate School of Business and the Research Center for Financial Engineering and Risk Management. For the last several years, I've made regular trips to Shanghai, Beijing and Hong Kong to meet with government leaders, entrepreneurs and investors in those regions.

Wright

What are your observations about how America stacks up against today's China?

Bodine

Today, we are ignoring a race between America and China that will affect us all for years to come. In broad terms, the world seems to have turned upside down since Richard Nixon first opened the door to a closed China over thirty years ago. Former NBA star Charles Barkley characterized the crazy times we live in when he said: "You know the world has turned upside down when the best basketball player in the world is Chinese, the best golfer is black, the best rapper is white and, as we learned recently just before the Iraq War, the Germans do not want to fight a war."

Wright

Charles Barkley always has something interesting to say, doesn't he? And I guess when you look at it that way, it does seem that the times have changed, not just in our country but all over the world.

Bodine

Exactly. And I think that sets the stage for my comparison of America and China and my insights into where the two countries stand in the world today. To do this, I suggest we look first are what makes a great country. As brief reference points, the historical examples of Rome, the Ottoman Empire and Great Britain are especially good. Also, a quick look at what led to their declines is very useful as we examine the situation today between America and China. Finally,

I want to talk about what I believe is going on in each country as we look at who's winning the race to dominate the 21st century.

The lessons of history clearly show that two major characteristics are required for a country to be great: economic power and political influence. History also shows that these two characteristics go together. With this said, perhaps a more important question to ask is: What causes great countries to decline? In the case of the Roman Empire, most historians identify the invasions from Germany as a prime cause for its decline. However, social, economic and political causes also had a great influence on the collapse of the Roman Empire.

Of these influences, the economic causes are most interesting, and these are startling as one thinks about America today. Let's look at these other factors that brought down Rome: (1) the decline in the work ethic; (2) the collapsing infrastructure of cities; (3) a large balance-of-trade deficit; (4) a burdensome cost of government, including military and welfare costs; (5) a class warfare between rich and poor; (6) the government became increasingly run by the rich and the military; and (7) citizens lost interest in government as it became more distant from them.

In the case of the Ottoman Empire, the dominant reason for its decline is that other powers, even their own neighbors, had grown stronger. Those neighbors also built stronger institutions and introduced more modern arms, infrastructure and better public administration. Perhaps the British Empire is the easiest decline to explain. In effect, Great Britain viewed itself in a paternalistic relationship with its colonies, while the colonies viewed England as a child molester. In the end, after nearly 200 years of global dominance, the subject countries of the British Empire demanded and received their independence.

Wright

Obviously, you must see some comparisons between these once-great empires and America's status as a superpower today.

Bodine

While I have no desire to stir up a political debate, I do want to highlight what I think are obvious facts about America today. I also want to note a few other facts that are less obvious unless you do some serious research to find them. First, it is clear that America is the largest and, most would agree, the strongest economic power in the world. I will come back to that in a minute. Second, our military strength, as evidenced in the latest Iraq War, is breathtaking. Of course, how we are doing now that we have "won the war" is an important question but not one for this discussion. Stay tuned. At a minimum, I think we are in for some ugly times ahead, and our recent problems with making peace in Iraq are, I believe, only the beginning. Nonetheless, in this analysis, no one should doubt that America is the greatest nation on earth.

Yet there is a great sense of unease in America today. A list of possible explanations is long and complicated, so let me only note a few facts that are contributing to the weakening of our great nation. First, any of us who have investments have suffered greatly in the last few years as the fixation on technology investing, extraordinary speculation on a staggering scale, unchecked corporate greed and corruption, and a loose regulatory environment have combined to wipe out trillions of dollars in our retirement savings. No American has gone untouched by this financial disaster.

Second, the explosive growth of complex financial instruments known as derivatives, led by America and now spread worldwide, alone represents, at latest count, well over $100 trillion in largely unregulated activity. I described this condition last spring to Chinese bankers as nothing less than "financial instruments of mass destruction." This time bomb is ticking and ticking loudly.

Third, the staggering amount of current fiscal debt in trillions of dollars is rising as our Congress recently voted to add an otherwise much-needed but costly drug benefit to Medicare beneficiaries while we are facing billions of dollars in unbudgeted military costs related to Iraq.

Fourth, there has been a massive withdrawal of billions of dollars in bank deposits from American banks as Middle East governments and their related private commercial interests react to the risk and record of America freezing bank deposits of perceived enemies in a changing world. Remember that a bank deposit has a multiplier effect of three or four to one throughout the entire financial system, and this is now gone and unlikely to return.

Fifth, the un-addressed but critical financial problem of our time is the coming Social Security crises that threatens each of you, your family and the country. I believe that our former Commerce Secretary, Pete Peterson, has done the best work on this issue. More could be said about the gap between the "haves" and the "have-nots." More could be shown about the decline of infrastructures in our cities. Particularly notable also are the financial disasters that most states are now experiencing, with no prospects for better times ahead. California's $38 billion deficit is the most glaring example, with staggering political and economic consequences. And more could be said about our trade imbalances. Even my good friend in New York, William Tehan, a brilliant investor and a keen observer of global financial affairs, points out that the Federal Reserve has lost control of our currency and that the Fed's recent efforts to help jump-start the U.S. economy have been in vain.

The picture I am suggesting should be clear: While our military power is unchallenged and our economic power, measured in absolute terms and relative to other major countries in the world, is the greatest history has ever recorded, America is deteriorating because of financial mismanagement at virtually all levels of government and in the private sector as well. This disturbing situation is largely a consequence of many of the same factors that led to the downfall of the great Roman Empire. Not only are the same signs visible in America, but such conditions are seriously undermining our economic and political strength in the world.

Wright

What about the flip side of the coin? How is China doing? I think that most Americans today have an image of China as being a repressed, impoverished nation that's probably still locked in the 20th century, at least from an economic standpoint.

Bodine

I think that to get a solid handle on China and its potential world impact, you first have to understand the sheer size of the country. China's population represents over sixteen percent of the total world population of 1.3 billion. It is a country whose growth in gross domestic product, measured in real terms, is currently running at a rate of well over seven percent, which is more than twice the rate of the U.S.

Wright

I'm not sure that most people are aware of that. What has contributed to that?

Bodine

Quite simply, China benefits from low labor costs, a commitment to high-quality goods and services, an enterprising population, ambitious leaders in both government and business and finally, flexible government policies that assist China as its seeks to dominate Asia. This is especially noteworthy as you consider that Japan struggles from the consequences of trying to rig its financial affairs in the world and getting caught, as it has in the past, in similar efforts to gain a global economic advantage. China also has shown enough progress to convince any rational observer that it seeks to become the dominant economic and military power in the latter part of the 21st century.

Wright

How far along are they in that quest?

Bodine

Assuming that current economic growth rates remain steady, China is expected to surpass the expected size of the U.S. economy—that's over $15 trillion—by 2018. What do I know from my work and my travels? First, anyone arriving today at the airport in Beijing, the political capital of China, would be stunned to see the newest and finest major airport in the world. Corridors of shops include the high-end goods from Cartier, Dunhill, Gucci and other chic global brands of the world. In Beijing itself, instead of finding a teeming sea of the great unwashed riding bicycles and looking poor, a visitor sees new cars and smiling people who are well dressed and working hard. Easy access to Western goods and services is visible everywhere: McDonald's, Starbucks, the Gap, etc. Yes, older people seem to be struggling, as they do everywhere else, including America. And, as I learned from my own daughter's six-month volunteer teaching experience last year in Wuhan—which is the Pittsburgh of China—many people in the outer cities, and especially the countryside, are quite poor. On the other hand, a visit to Shanghai, the economic capital—not unlike our New York City—also finds one in "shock and awe" of that city's extraordinary new, magnificent skyline that reflects a brilliant combination and careful integration of the world's finest architectural creations. It is truly the most impressive skyline anywhere in the world today. However, whether visiting Beijing or Shanghai, you come away with a clear vision that the Chinese feel a sense of destiny, excitement and perhaps inevitability in their progress toward becoming the major global power of the 21st century.

Wright

What exactly is the driving force behind China's progress and success?

Bodine

First, China is a vast country with massive resources. Some things, such as oil, are needed, but generally, China, like Russia and America, enjoys great capabilities in raw materials. Second, the Chinese work very hard. They are very smart and are rapidly learning Western ways. Importantly, they are avoiding our mistakes. Third, their Communist leaders have been brilliant in allowing experiments and then writing new rules and regulations to make things work better. To be sure, they are ruthless in their efforts to maintain power, control the country and manage its progress in converting from an agricultural society to a balanced, global, economic powerhouse. That ruthlessness will not change, as we saw in Tianenman Square in the late 1980s. They also know history. They study, understand and possess a very clear vision of world affairs. They think very long term and rarely make mistakes. To be sure, they are in a hurry to catch up with America but never at the expense of their long-term economic and political goals. Will they test us? Of course they will and have already. For example, what the U.S called a "mapping error," which led to the precision bombing of the Chinese embassy in Belgrade, I believe represented a strong U.S. response to Chinese interference in the war in Kosovo.

Wright

Over the years, I've heard various news reports that talk about how the United States has even helped contribute to the strengthening of China as a world power. Is this true?

Bodine

At the trade level, the answer is quite obviously "yes." Americans are buying massive amounts of goods from China, saving money on low-priced Chinese goods and also finding that the Chinese are much like the Koreans—the best copiers of any item in the world, including the most chic and expensive handbags made by Hermes of Paris. The differences are virtually undetectable, and the bags are sold at one tenth the price of the real ones in Paris.

At another level, until September 11, 2001, we allowed the best young minds and talented students of China to come to the best universities in America to learn and then return to China to apply their newfound understanding. In many instances, these exceptional young people return as highly paid employees of U.S. companies doing business in China. Others return home as new leaders in the new economy of the PRC. A fourth driving force are the policies of a strong central government of leaders, who are now younger and possess more intelligence, know-how and winning strategies than ever before and apply them to almost anything they want to accomplish. Finally, the Chinese are brilliant at seizing opportunities and exploiting the weaknesses of others, whether they're temporary problems, in the case of Japan, or the more serious long-term problems facing America.

Wright

It almost makes you wonder about Nixon's relationship with China back in the seventies. If he could have foreseen what would happen there in the decades to come, I wonder if he would have been so eager to normalize relations.

Bodine

As bright as Richard Nixon was and as brilliant a visionary as he was in opening the door to China in 1972, it is unlikely that he foresaw the Grand Dragon that China is becoming— ironically, at our expense. Whether or not China's military vision of its role in the world will ultimately collide with the American Eagle, as most conservative observers believe will happen, is an open question. However, what is clear is that the Chinese now sell more weapons of mass destruction than anyone in the world, a fact that does not go unnoticed by the U.S. Under the new Bush foreign doctrine, it is predictable that such activity will likely be confronted, at least with those who are buying Chinese arms.

Perhaps, in others ways, China can be slowed. For example, some have suggested that the recent SARS problem in China was the result of a CIA special operations effort to plant the disease in order to slow their economic growth. We will likely never know the real source of SARS. Neither the CIA nor the Chinese will disclose what they know. Nevertheless, what is clear is that China, with or without SARS, will likely be the Grand Dragon of the late 21st century. Breathing fire or not, that case can be made. At least for now, let me suggest that the Chinese are the fastest out of the gate in the race to dominate the late 21st century and to change the world as we now know it.

Wright

Where do you see things going from here?

Bodine

Looking at the big picture, our country will be more focused on national security issues for the next five to ten years than on economic development and providing the most favorable opportunities for entrepreneurs. I do not see that changing. If anything, we will find ourselves being more concerned as the dynamics of what's going on in Iraq unfold in the future. I'm not optimistic that the key people in our current administration have an understanding that translates into America being effective in its objectives in that region. The consequences will require that we spend a lot more time, money and energy on security than on business.

On the other hand, the Chinese have a great advantage because of their distance—literally halfway around the world. They also have a big advantage because of their general environment. They're relatively free of the national security issues that we face in the West. China's dominant mentality is to succeed in business activities, and it's happening at a stunning pace. They're being very smart about policies, and I don't see that changing for at least the next ten to fifteen years. I compare it to the California gold rush of the 1850s. China has gigantic business opportunities. The scale and magnitude of what can be done is staggering.

Wright

If capitalism is gaining such a strong foothold, is it likely to bring about political change in China in the long term?

Bodine

What's been remarkable at the governmental level is that you have a transition from the old guard to the younger leadership. The old guard is being phased out, and the newer generation is moving forward. This new generation is very sophisticated in understanding the West. Many of them are very educated and received their educations in the West. They're still a part of the communist party, but they appreciate the capitalism of the West. They're allowing experiments to help capitalism to develop at all levels, and they're rewriting the rules to sustain those efforts.

Of course, for now, they still maintain very careful controls so things don't get out of hand; I don't see that changing. But imagine trying to run a country with 1.3 billion people. You could never have enough police forces to maintain complete control over the people, so you have to allow them to move forward and have some satisfactions and comforts in life. What is happening is that the eastern section of the country is in a state of dramatic business development. In the middle section of the country, the people are desperate to survive, so you see a lot of movement to the coastal regions in order to make money and survive.

China's leaders have watched very carefully what went on in Russia and successfully avoided the mistakes the Russians made in terms of having an economic free-for-all, which resulted in just a few people making billions of dollars. I don't think that will happen with the Chinese, because they have been very controlled in the pace of the development of their country.

Wright

Could the changes going on in China ultimately lead to a democratic society?

Bodine

Democracy definitely has a foothold there now. It's pervasive in their thinking, especially in the eastern coastal regions. There's no question that people will want a bigger say in how things are done, but it's an evolutionary process, not a revolutionary process; a revolution is not necessary. In my view, it will succeed, because you have a government that is allowing it to succeed in stages and people who are enjoying the success of that incremental progress toward more material benefits and a better life.

Wright

What should our focus be in America? It seems to me that we should put more effort into bolstering our own strengths.

Bodine

We've got to get our financial house in order at all levels. We need to be honest in our accounting practices at the government level and stop using financial gimmicks and mirrors that create the illusion of stability and financial order. What's going on has been a complete farce. At the corporate level, a good deal has to be cleaned up as well. Companies have more debt than they should, and at the consumer level, we're seeing a shocking level of financial overextension, which is driven by excess borrowing. So we've got to get our house in order financially as a country. If the government didn't keep printing money, we'd have a financial disaster at the governmental level.

Wright

Wow. You've certainly given us some sobering possibilities to consider today, Bill. And I can't believe our time is up already. We've been talking today with William Bodine, chairman of The Investment Advisory Group, a company that provides strategic investment and consulting services to major institutions as well as significant product groups, individuals and governments throughout world.

Bill founded his own company after managing a similar venture under the auspices of his previous employer, the J.P. Morgan company. Prior to that, he was director of investment research for Citicorp's Global Investment Management Group. He also worked with the College Retirement Equities Fund and was a vice president of research for Scudder, Stevens and Clark.

Some of Bill's other career highlights, which weren't mentioned earlier, include his service as Senior Capital Markets Advisor to the Republic of Kazhakstan and as risk-management advisor to the Industrial Finance Corporation of Thailand. He has taught at both Oxford University and lectured at the Harvard Business School, where his pioneering work in the discipline of asset management is well documented.

Bill, this has been a fascinating conversation. I wish we had more time to continue.

Bodine

David, I've enjoyed it. I appreciate your having me on the show today.

About The Author

Dr. A. William Bodine is a globally recognized investment advisor and industry leader whose accomplishments in and understanding of the "global village" have made him one of the most sought after motivational leaders in the world. His professional experience as Chairman of The Investment Advisory Group including current positions as Chairman of The China Mantou Fund, Chairman of The Russian Blue chip Fund, previous senior executive positions at J.P. Morgan and Citicorp Investment Management, leadership of the most important professional associations (AIMR, NYSSA, ISFA and FAF), civic and Church organizations in the US and abroad prove his remarkable motivating skills in providing effective leadership in today's global village.

A. William Bodine, Ph.D.
Chairman of The Investment Advisory Group
67 Wall Street - Suite #2211
New York, New York 10005
Phone: USA 011. 212.726.2300
Fax: USA 011.212.591.6748
E-mail: USA BodineUno@aol.com

Chapter 18

PHILLIP VAN HOOSER, MBA, CSP

THE INTERVIEW

David E. Wright (Wright)

Today we're talking with Phillip Van Hooser. He talks about leadership and you can tell he has walked his talk. The first ten years of Phil's career were spent working as a human resources manager in FORTUNE 500 manufacturing facilities around the United States. His solid leadership foundation was laid as he worked to help supervisors and managers evolve from traditional authoritarian management styles to the more progressive participative leadership styles that are being practiced today.

In 1988, Phillip expanded his vision by founding Van Hooser Associates. Since that time, Phil has developed and presented over 2,300 leadership development programs for more than 700 corporate and association clients such as S.E. Johnson Wax, KFC, the International Association of City Managers, BellSouth, the City of Phoenix and the United States Army.

Known for his common sense insight, real world experience and practical applications, Phil's programs on leadership, team building and service professionalism issues have assisted developing leaders and helped transform businesses across America and beyond. Phil has created and produced four audio/video training series, *Learning to Lead, Common Sense Leadership, The Leadership Challenge* and *The Leadership Journey: Practical Skills for Leadership Success.* In 1999, Phil penned and published *You're Joe's Boy, Ain't Ya? Life's Lessons for Living, Loving and Leading,* an inspirational collection of leadership lessons learned on the way from childhood to adulthood. In January, 2004, Phil's newest book, *It Takes More Than Guts* will be released.

Phil is an active member of the 3,500 member National Speakers Association where he is currently serving on the national Board of Directors. Phil, his wife, Susan and their three children make their home in Princeton, Kentucky. Phil, welcome to *Conversations on Leadership.*

Phillip Van Hooser (Van Hooser)

Thank you, David.

Wright

Phil, why are there so few leaders and so many followers in our world today?

Van Hooser

David, without question many people believe that it is easier and less risky to follow than it is to lead. Following doesn't require them to invest as much of themselves in an activity. Followers don't have to think as much, plan as much and put as much on the line. When all is said and done, they can always point fingers at someone else and say, "It's not my fault. He/she told me to do it" or "He/she should have done it... ." Let's face it, it's easier to second guess than it is to take the lead.

But, for those who see the benefit of accepting a leadership role, specifically the readers you are reaching, most would agree that leadership can be an extremely rewarding process. Leadership teaches us much. It provides many unique opportunities. Most importantly, it helps us make a difference in the businesses and communities in which we work and live, through the people with whom we work and live.

Wright

How would you define leadership?

Van Hooser

David, leadership continues to evolve for me. For example, I used to share the following leadership definition with my clients and audiences: The successful leader is the one who can get the group to accomplish established goals, with the least amount of friction, while maintaining the greatest sense of unity and yet still providing individual self-realization.

Wright

That's kind of a high-brow definition, isn't it?

Van Hooser

Absolutely. It should come as no big surprise that I was working on my MBA degree about the time I coined that definition. It may have served as a good answer to some essay question posed in some Masters level management class, but relative to practical leadership application, it served no worthwhile purpose at all.

Wright

Okay, so what is a more practical and realistic leadership definition?

Van Hooser

After years of observation, countless conversations with respected leaders and feedback from hundreds of conscientious followers who have shared with me what they respect and appreciate about their leaders, I came up with a new definition of leadership. It consists of two primary things. Number one, leadership is the ability to offer service. Number two, leadership is the willingness to take action.

Service first. In America, we are a consumer-driven economy. We buy, sell and utilize the products and services of various suppliers and vendors every day. As a result, we have learned that good service means meeting and occasionally exceeding our expectations.

I would argue that the same concept holds true between a leader and his or her followers. In other words, followers have certain expectations of their leaders. If those expectations are met and satisfied, these followers have a tendency to follow passionately, for extended periods. On the other hand, if a follower's expectations are not met by their leader, there is certain to be a breakdown of confidence after which any number of problems may occur.

As for the willingness to take action, I truly believe that with a moderate amount of thought, consideration and observation, most prospective leaders can accurately determine what their followers expect of them. At that point, it simply becomes an act of follow through. If we fail to act—to follow through—we in essence sabotage our leadership potential in the eyes of our followers. The end result is that they can't trust or respect us, because we haven't made the effort to do all that we can do as leaders to earn their trust and respect.

Wright

That brings me to my next question. What do you see as being the difference between a leader and a manager?

Van Hooser

I think there is a definite distinction between leadership and management. Yet, many people work for years in their careers without recognizing the difference. I think I know why that is.

In my own case, I have an undergraduate degree in Marketing Management. I have earned my Masters of Business Administration degree with a concentration in management. I worked for the first ten years of my career as a manager in FORTUNE 500 organizations. In other words, I have spent thousands of dollars and thousands of hours learning the fine art of planning, controlling, directing and organizing things. That's what I believe most of us were taught.

Wright

Absolutely.

Van Hooser

I went on to learn that what we, as managers, needed to plan, control, direct and organize were resources and that there are four basic resource groups that would require my continuous attention. Physical resources included facilities, equipment, fleets and so forth. Financial resources included budgets, revenue, profits and the like. Technological resources would include electronic communications, commerce and various record keeping activities.

Now, David, I realize I said that there are four resource groups. But, let me quickly review these first three. Any of the three, whether it's physical, financial or technological resources, are no more than just things. Things to be planned for; things to be controlled; things to be directed; and things to be organized. These all justify management activities.

But the fourth resource group—human resources—are more than things. We're talking about people. People that need to be led, not managed. Physical, financial and technological resources cannot think for themselves. They must be managed. Not so with people. Individuals make dozens of independent decisions every day—regardless of the specific positions they occupy. One of the most important decisions they will consciously and continuously make is this, "Will I follow this person or not? If so, why? If not, why not?"

David, I sometimes ask my clients the following question. In your professional careers, whether they span three years or thirty-three years, can you identify the single most important professional decision that you've made? Since, in the course of a career, they've probably made tens of thousands of decisions, you would probably agree that this particular question is a tough one to answer.

Wright

It sure is.

Van Hooser

Well, I've thought about that question regarding my own professional career. I have considered a number of important decisions that have shaped my career over time. I decided to pursue a particular educational degree. I decided to go to work for one company and then another. I decided to accept a promotion and then a transfer at different times. I decided to start my own company. I decided to write books.

As important as these and many other decisions I've made have proven to be, I am convinced none of them was my most important professional decision. For me, the single most important decision I've ever made was determining that I wanted to be a leader not a manager. From that critical decision my entire professional focus changed.

Please understand that I don't intend to disrespect the position of management. Management is necessary for things. But, once I decided to be a leader my focus was fixed on learning the fine art of influencing and impacting people. It has made all the difference for me. That is why I am so passionate about the leadership message and lessons I share.

Wright

So what characteristics should leaders possess?

Van Hooser

Over the past twelve years or so, I have made a point of asking my audience members to recall the most effective leader they had ever known and what characteristic he or she possessed that made them so effective. In return, I have collected the various characteristics they have identified. David, would you believe that I have received more than 270 different leadership characteristics as identified by my program participants?

Wright

Wow!

Van Hooser

Now, that's exactly how I have felt for the past dozen years—wow!

Wright

I would have thought the number to be maybe 50.

Van Hooser

That sounds more reasonable to me, too. But, I continue to learn that different people see and focus on different things. But, if I try to tell my audiences that to be an effective leader they must learn and practice 270 leadership skills, most people would just throw up their hands and quit trying right there. It is just too much for almost anyone to comprehend.

But, I've also learned that some leadership characteristics are primary and others secondary. I'll give you an example. There is one characteristic that is mentioned almost every time I address the issue of leadership characteristics publicly. By far, it is mentioned more than any other characteristic. Any idea what it might be?

Wright

May I guess, honesty?

Van Hooser

David, that's a wonderful guess. If there had been a prize you would have just won it. Not only is honesty mentioned with great regularity, but often it is the very first characteristic that is identified as we start to create our list. Over time, I have come to realize that people value honesty in their leaders over just about everything else. In other words, you or I can be deficient in some other leadership characteristics and people will probably forgive or overlook the deficiency. But, if we are lacking honesty, people simply can't overlook that. It is one of the key foundations of personal leadership.

David, you may be interested to know that I have found the other two most common characteristics behind honesty to be integrity and trust.

Wright

Don't you wish various leaders would recognize this fact?

Van Hooser

David, it's amazing. The news constantly trumpets the reports of terrible leadership decisions that have been made and the horrible outcomes that are experienced as a result of them in governments, in businesses, in families, and so on.

Wright

Phil, what is the difference between "honesty" and "integrity?" Aren't they really describing the same thing?

Van Hooser

David, if they were the same thing we wouldn't need two different words to describe them. However, they are closely related. I refer to them as first cousins—related, but with their own identity. Let me try to explain.

Honesty is about truth, candor and forthrightness. Integrity is certainly all those things, but still slightly different. I have a personal definition for integrity. I tell my audiences that integrity is doing the right thing, because it is the right thing to do—not because it is the easy thing, or the quick thing, or even the politically correct thing—but because it is the right to do.

Sometimes I am asked if, by my definition, honesty and integrity can contradict or run contrary to one another. Let me give you an example of how they might seem contradictory and yet still be able to coexist beneficially.

I've sat in meetings where the discussion revolved around a problem that is being experienced with an individual. For extended periods we wrestle with how to handle this particular person and the situation that has been created? Suddenly, someone gets frustrated and says something like this, "Why are we wasting all this time? We all know what the problem is. If no one else will handle this matter, I will." With that, they are on their feet and out of the room they go. A few minutes later they return, smiling proudly and exclaim, "There. I handled that. I told him exactly how things were going to be."

David, I ask you, is the problem resolved or have we potentially created a whole new set of problems? Only time will tell. But, one thing is for sure. In a matter of minutes, through an act of brutal honesty, a relationship that may have taken days, weeks, months or even years to develop may be irreparably damaged. Integrity asks, what is the right thing to do at this moment? What are the possible outcomes of brutal honesty versus a more cautious and thoughtful integrity-based approach? Consider this simple example:

Someone walks up to you and thrusts a picture of a newborn baby in your face while exclaiming, "Look at my baby, isn't she beautiful?" You take one look at the picture and you think to yourself, that is absolutely the ugliest baby I have ever seen!

Wright

All newborns look like Winston Churchill.

Van Hooser

(laughing) You're exactly right. But is it wise to look at that parent or grandparent who is obviously proud of this new arrival and say, "That baby is so ugly you're going to have to tie a pork chop to it to get the dog to play with her?"

Wright

(laughing) I don't think that would be too wise.

Van Hooser

Exactly. You're not going to do that because you know it would devastate them. You also know that they will become defensive and that you probably will have created an unnecessary confrontation. You're also not going to lie. Honesty is still paramount. Instead, you will probably opt for the integrity-based response by saying something like, "Oh, all babies are gifts from God—every child a blessing" or "isn't it wonderful to consider the potential that a new life possesses?" That person will walk away satisfied, even though you didn't say the child was the prettiest you had ever seen. You didn't believe that. They were encouraged because you made an effort to build without first tearing down.

Wright

A wise man once told me, "David, if you consider yourself a leader and you look behind you and no one is following you—then you're just out for a walk."

Van Hooser

That's something we all need to remember.

Wright

So, how does a leader go about earning someone's respect?

Van Hooser

We all know that respect is critical. Whether it is an adult being respected by a child, a teacher by a student, an employer by an employee or a company by its customers, respect is critical. Yet, as important as it is, I fear that too few people take the time to analyze and therefore understand how to go about earning respect. Most people think that earning respect is as simple as granting respect to others. It's not that easy. As you have already indicated, respect must be earned. I like to tell my audiences that there is a "recipe" for earning respect that consists of three very important ingredients.

Wright

Would you share those three ingredients with us?

Van Hooser

Sure. The first ingredient to earning respect is consistency. That should be obvious, but I'm not sure it is. How could we ever expect others to respect and follow our lead if we are inconsistent in word, deed and actions? Inconsistency gives the undeniable perception of a poor leader. Followers will adapt and adjust their behavior based on the actions of their leader. Inconsistent behavior on the part of the leader simply causes confusion and ultimately chaos in the ranks of followers because they are constantly confused as to what they should be adapting and adjusting to. Leaders have to be able to clearly communicate who they are, what they believe and what they are working toward.

Wright

Consistency sounds like a solid foundation from which to earn respect. What about the second ingredient?

Van Hooser

Of equal importance to consistency in earning respect is the ability to make quality decisions. David, notice I said "quality" decisions, I didn't say "perfect" decisions. In my opinion, there is no such thing as a perfect decision without having perfect knowledge of the future. None of us do. Therefore, you will make mistakes. But, mistakes need not destroy the respect others have for you. Not if you handle mistakes properly. Two things to remember: once mistakes have been made, take responsibility for them quickly and publicly. If you take responsibility quickly, but only share your mistake with a select few, people won't respect you. If you take responsibility publicly, but delay in doing so, then people won't trust you regardless of what you confess to. To earn respect, fess up when you mess up—without delay!

Wright

That makes sense to me. What's the third ingredient?

Van Hooser

The third ingredient is the ability to get along with others—especially those who act or think differently than us. I appreciate a quote attributed to Abraham Lincoln. Lincoln said, "I don't like that man—I think I need to get to know him better." If we are really interested in earning the respect of those we come in contact with personally or professionally we need to look and work past our differences and difficulties to find our common ground. In so doing, we earn the respect of others who are not ready or able to do the same.

Wright

That's a very interesting and practical way to view the process of earning respect.

Van Hooser

Thank you. It works for me. I know it can work for others as well.

Wright

Phil, you have given us a lot of good information about leadership. But, if you had to boil it all down, is there one essential element of leadership that you could share with us?

Van Hooser

David, I think there is. Very simply put, the essential element of leadership is followers. I am certain that some well-meaning individuals never recognize this point. With good intentions, I might add, they try to make mission statements, or charisma, or even reporting relationships the central theme in establishing their leadership. These are all good. But, the essential element of good leadership has been, is, and always will be having the focus clearly fixed on the followers. Once a trust-based relationship has been established between follower and leader, then and only then will these other things start to have a great impact. Several years ago, a participant in one of my leadership workshops gave me a cartoon. It depicted a guy laboring severely as he ran up hill. The caption beneath the cartoon read, "There they go down the road and I must run and catch them—for I am their leader!" I wonder how many of our readers have ever felt that way. If you ever have felt that way, you certainly know that there is nothing laughable about the situation. Getting to know your followers and what they need from you as their leader is critical.

Wright

Phil, I've been on a church staff for about 40 years and I have led a number of different companies. Nevertheless, there has been something that has continuously baffled me. I love to interact with people. As a leader, I've been told all kinds of things. Let me get your opinion. How close should leaders be to their followers?

Van Hooser

That is a very important question and you summed it up nicely. We've all been told different things as we have attempted to learn specific leadership skills. Sometimes the information and advice is good. But, David, we must also recognize that sometimes the information and advice we receive is bad. Early in my career, I was advised by people more senior and seasoned than me that I shouldn't get too close to the people I was attempting to lead. They explained their reasoning this way. If I got too close to the people, when it came time to make a difficult professional decision regarding them, I wouldn't be able to separate my personal feelings toward them from my professional responsibilities. Therefore, it would just be easier not to get close to them at all.

Wright

I've certainly heard that.

Van Hooser

Unfortunately, too many of us have heard this. I think it is a terribly short-sighted and misleading perspective. I take a fundamentally different approach. This is exactly what I tell my client groups. You *can* be a *manager* without getting close to your people. It happens every day. Managers love to manage *things*—not *people*. On the other hand, you can't be a leader *unless* you get close to people. Consider this question. Why in the world would some consciously choose to follow someone who has intentionally not taken time to get to know them or to show some interest in them? When I suggest getting to know them—I'm not talking about dating them, or going on vacation with them or having them over for cookouts every weekend—I am talking about getting to know them for who they are, understanding their hopes, their dreams, their aspirations, but also understanding their fears, anxieties and concerns. Let's face it, the more a leader knows about his or her follower, the more successful he or she is going to be in relating to that follower as they work and grow together.

Wright

Well, I tell you, Phil, this has been a great conversation. I have really learned some important things from our time together. I appreciate the time you have taken with me as we have considered these important aspects of leadership together.

Van Hooser

David, it has been a real privilege for me to be able to share my thoughts with you. I wish we could have spent more time together.

Wright

We have been talking with Phillip Van Hooser. His firm, Van Hooser Associates, Inc. is dedicated to helping individuals and organizations enhance their leadership potential. I think he has done that for us here. For more information on Phil and the services he offers, visit www.VanHooser.com. Thanks again, Phil.

Van Hooser

It was my pleasure.

About The Author

Phillip Van Hooser KNOWS what people want from their leaders. From his experience as a FORTUNE 500 manager, Van Hooser shows managers and executives how to motivate their people, how to cultivate employee loyalty–how to become a leader their people want to follow! A keynote speaker, leadership trainer and author, Van Hooser has transformed leaders across the U.S. and beyond with his practical experience and insight.

Phillip Van Hooser, MBA, CSP
PO Box 643
Princeton, Kentucky 42445
Phone: 800.236.6765
Phone: 270.365.1536
Fax: 270.365.6678
Email: phil@vanhooser.com
www.vanhooser.com